Rick Steves®

SNAPSHOT

Lisbon

CONTENTS

INTRODUCTION

This Snapshot guide, excerpted from my guidebook *Rick Steves Portugal,* introduces you to Lisbon, the country's culturally rich capital. Here at the far western edge of Europe, prices are reasonable, the people are warm, and the pace of life slows. Wander through Lisbon's characteristic downtown neighborhoods like the hilly Alfama and the busy Baixa, then head up to the lanes of Bairro Alto at night to find a good fado bar. The grand Belém district offers a look at Lisbon's historic architecture and seafaring glory, from the 16th-century Monastery of Jerónimos to the Monument to the Discoveries. Visit the Gulbenkian Museum, the best of Lisbon's 40 museums, offering 5,000 years' worth of art.

Day-trip to the touristy but lovely town of Sintra, dotted with the fanciful Pena Palace, royal National Palace, and evocative Moorish castle ruins atop a hill.

To help you have the best trip possible, I've included the following topics in this book:

• **Planning Your Time,** with advice on how to make the most of your limited time

• **Orientation,** including tourist information (abbreviated as TI), tips on public transportation, local tour options, and helpful hints

• **Sights** with ratings:

▲▲▲—Don't miss

▲▲—Try hard to see

▲—Worthwhile if you can make it

No rating—Worth knowing about

• **Sleeping** and **Eating,** with good-value recommendations in every price range

• **Transportation Connections,** with tips on trains, buses, and driving

Practicalities, near the end of this book, has information on money, phoning, hotel reservations, transportation, and more, plus Portuguese survival phrases.

To travel smartly, read this little book in its entirety before you go. It's my hope that this guide will make your trip more meaningful and rewarding. Traveling like a temporary local, you'll get the absolute most out of every mile, minute, and dollar.

Boa-viagem!

Rick Steves

LISBON

Lisboa

Lisbon is a ramshackle but charming mix of now and then. Vintage trolleys shiver up and down its hills, bird-stained statues mark grand squares, taxis rattle and screech through cobbled lanes, and well-worn people sip coffee in Art Nouveau cafés. It's a city of faded ironwork balconies, multicolored tiles, and mosaic sidewalks, of bougainvillea and red-tiled roofs with antique TV antennas. Men in suits and billed caps offer to "plastify" your documents, and Africans in traditional garb sell gemstones from handkerchiefs spread on sidewalks.

Lisbon, Portugal's capital, is the country's banking and manufacturing center. Residents call their city Lisboa (leezh-BOH-ah), which comes from the Phoenician term *Alis Ubbo,* meaning "calm port." A port city on the yawning mouth of the Rio Tejo (Tagus River), Lisbon welcomes large ships to its waters and state-of-the-art dry docks. And it's becoming a popular stop with cruise ships.

Romans and Moors originally populated Lisbon, but the city's glory days were in the 15th and 16th centuries, when explorers such as Vasco da Gama opened new trade routes around Africa to India, making Lisbon one of Europe's richest cities. Portugal's Age of Discovery fueled rapid economic growth, which sparked the flamboyant art boom called the Manueline period—named after King Manuel I (r. 1495-1521). In the 17th and 18th centuries, the gold, diamonds, and sugarcane of Brazil (one of Portugal's colonies) made Lisbon even wealthier.

Then, on the morning of All Saints' Day in 1755, while most of the population was at church, a tremendous underwater earthquake occurred off the southern Portuguese coast. The violent se-

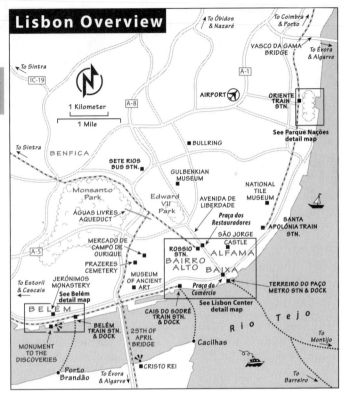

ries of tremors were felt throughout Europe—as far away as Finland. Two-thirds of Lisbon was leveled. Fires—started by cooking flames and church candles—raged through the wooden city center, and a huge tsunami caused by the earthquake blasted the waterfront. Imagine a disaster similar to 2004's Indian Ocean earthquake and tsunami, devastating Portugal's capital city.

Under the energetic and eventually dictatorial leadership of Prime Minister Marquês de Pombal—who had the new city planned within a month of the quake—downtown Lisbon was rebuilt on a progressive grid plan, with broad boulevards and generous squares. Remnants of Lisbon's pre-earthquake charm survive in Belém, the Alfama, and the Bairro Alto district. The bulk of your sightseeing will likely be in these neighborhoods.

As the Paris of the Portuguese-speaking world, Lisbon (pop. 548,000 in the core) is the Old World capital of its former empire—for some 100 million people stretching from Europe to Brazil to Africa to China. Immigrants from former colonies such as Mozambique and Angola have added diversity and flavor to the

Pronunciation Guide to Lisbon

Lisboa	leezh-BOH-ah
Rossio (main square)	roh-SEE-oo
Praça da Figueira (major square)	PRAH-sah dah fee-GAY-rah
Baixa (lower town)	BYE-shah
Alfama (hilly neighborhood)	al-FAH-mah
Bairro Alto (high town)	BYE-roh AHL-too
Chiado (part of Bairro Alto)	shee-AH-doo
Belém (suburb with sights)	bay-LEHM
Rio Tejo (Tagus River)	REE-oo TAY-zhoo
rua (street)	ROO-ah

city, making it as likely that you'll hear African music as Portuguese fado these days.

With its characteristic hills, trolleys, famous suspension bridge, and rolling fog, Lisbon has a San Francisco feel. And Lisbon's heritage survives. Enjoy all this world-class city has to offer, from its elegant outdoor cafés, exciting art, stunning vistas, and entertaining museums, to the salty sailors' quarter with its hill-capping castle.

PLANNING YOUR TIME

For a two-week tour of Portugal, Lisbon is worth three days, including perhaps a day for a side-trip to Sintra. If you have an extra day, there's plenty to do.

Note that many top sights are closed on Monday, particularly in Belém. That'd be a good day to choose among the following options: Take my self-guided neighborhood walks; day-trip to Sintra (where all of the major sights are open); go on a guided walking tour with Lisbon Walker or Inside Lisbon; or head to Parque das Nações for a dose of modern Lisbon.

Day 1: See Lisbon's three downtown neighborhoods (following my self-guided "Three Neighborhoods" Walk): Alfama, Baixa, and Bairro Alto. Start where the city did, at its castle (hop a taxi to get there at 9:00 before the crowds hit). After surveying the city from the highest viewpoint in town, you'll take the walk downhill into the characteristic Alfama neighborhood and end at the Fado Museum. From there, zip over to the big main square (Praça do Comércio) to begin exploring the Baixa ("lower town"). That walk takes you through the major squares, Praça da Figueira and Rossio. Then ride up the Elevador da Glória funicular to begin the Bairro Alto and Chiado walk. Art lovers can then hop a taxi to the Gulbenkian Museum (open until 18:00, closed Mon). Consider dinner at a fado show in the Bairro Alto or the Alfama. For more evening options, see "Entertainment in Lisbon" and "Shopping in Lisbon" (malls/cinemas are open late).

Day 2: Trolley to Belém and tour the monastery, tower, and National Coach Museum. Have lunch in Belém or across the river in Porto Brandão, then tour the Museum of Ancient Art on your way back to Lisbon.

Day 3: Side-trip to Sintra to tour the Pena Palace and explore the ruined Moorish castle.

Orientation to Lisbon

Downtown Lisbon fills a valley flanked by two hills along the banks of the Rio Tejo. At the heart sits the main square, **Rossio,** in the center of the valley (with Praça dos Restauradores and Praça da Figueira nearby). The **Baixa,** or lower town, stretches from Rossio to the waterfront. It's a flat, pleasant shopping area of grid-patterned streets and the pedestrian-only Rua Augusta. The **Alfama,** the hill to the east, is a colorful tangle of medieval streets, topped by São Jorge Castle. The **Bairro Alto** ("high town"), the hill to the west, has characteristic old lanes on the top and high-fashion stores along Rua Garrett (in the lower section called **Chiado**).

From Rossio, the **modern city** stretches north (sloping uphill) along wide Avenida da Liberdade and beyond (way beyond), where you find Edward VII Park, breezy botanical gardens, the bullring, and the airport. To the east is **Parque das Nações,** site of the 1998 World Expo and now a modern shopping complex and riverfront promenade. The suburb of Belém, home to several Age of Discovery sights, is three miles west of the city, along the waterfront.

Greater Lisbon has more than three million people and some frightening sprawl, but for the visitor, the old city center is your target—a delightful series of parks, boulevards, and squares in a crusty, well-preserved architectural shell. Focus on the three characteristic neighborhoods that line the downtown harborfront: the Alfama, Baixa, and Bairro Alto.

TOURIST INFORMATION

Lisbon has several tourist offices—all branded "ask me Lisboa"—and additional information kiosks sprout around town late each spring. The main TIs are: on **Praça dos Restauradores** at Palácio Foz (daily 9:00-20:00, tel. 213-463-314; TI for rest of Portugal in same office, tel. 218-494-323 or 213-463-658); on **Praça do Comércio** (daily 9:00-20:00, tel. 210-312-810); and at the **airport** (daily 7:00-24:00, especially helpful, tel. 218-450-660). Small TI kiosks are at the **Santa Apolónia train station** (Tue-Sat 7:30-9:30, closed Sun-Mon, toward the end of track 3) and in front of the monastery in **Belém** (Tue-Sat 10:00-13:00 & 14:00-18:00, closed Sun-Mon, tel. 213-658-435).

Each TI offers handy freebies including a Lisbon city map (with helpful inset of town center), an in-depth *Public Transport Guide* (showing bus, Metro, and trolley lines in detail), and the monthly *Follow Me Lisboa* magazine (monthly, mainly cultural and museum listings). If you want a LisboaCard (described next), buy it at a TI. Good websites for information are www.insidelisbon.com, www.visitlisboa.com (click on "Publications" to find the *Follow Me Lisboa* magazine as a free PDF), and www.visitportugal.com.

LisboaCard: This card covers all public transportation (as well as trains to Sintra and Cascais) and free entry to many museums (including the Museum of Ancient Art, National Tile Museum, National Coach Museum, Monastery of Jerónimos, and Bélem Tower, plus some Sintra sights). It also provides discounts on many museums, city tours, and river cruises.

You can buy the card at Lisbon's TIs (including the airport TI), but not at participating sights. If you plan to museum-hop, the card is a good value, particularly for a day in Belém (covers your transportation and most sightseeing). Don't get the card for Sunday, when many sights are free until 14:00, or for Monday, when many sights are closed. The card is also unnecessary if you're a student or senior, for whom most sights are free or half-price.

The LisboaCard is straightforward and can save you well over €25 if you do everything suggested in my three-day plan for Lisbon. Carry the LisboaCard booklet with you when you sightsee; some discounts require coupons contained inside, plus it serves as a proof of purchase (€19/24 hours, €32/48 hours, €39/72 hours, kids 5-11 half-price, includes excellent explanatory guidebook, www.askmelisboa.com).

ARRIVAL IN LISBON

Information on arriving in Lisbon by plane, train, bus, cruise ship, and car follows. A helpful website is www.golisbon.com/transport. If you have a little money and/or are traveling with a group, simply hop in a taxi upon arrival—they're plentiful and cheap (except at the cruise terminals; see warning later). You can get from the airport or train station to your hotel for under €10 by taxi.

By Plane

Lisbon's easy-to-manage Portela Airport is five miles northeast of downtown (airport code: LIS; for airport info, call 218-413-500 or TAP Portugal at tel. 707-205-700). While you're at the airport,

LISBON

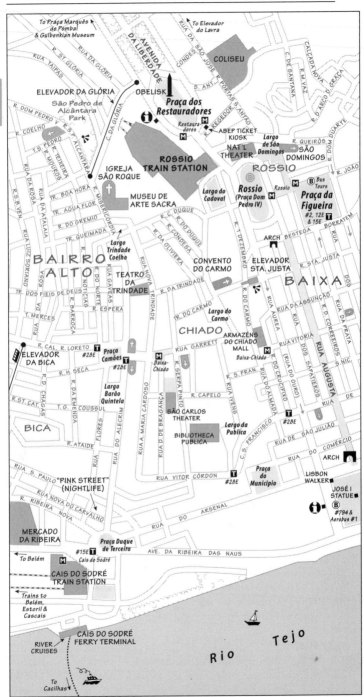

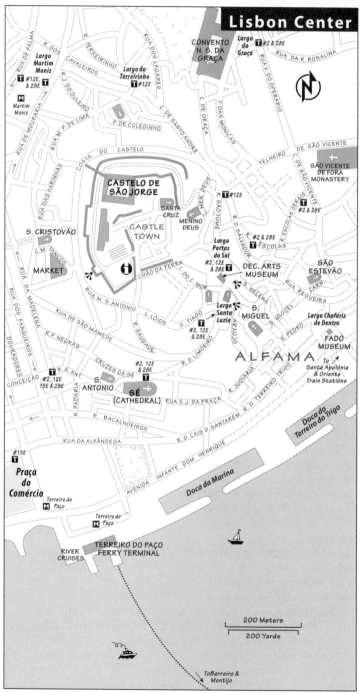

Lisbon Center

CONVENTO N. S. DA GRAÇA

Largo da Graça · #2 & 28E

RUA DA R. ROSALINA

Largo Martim Moniz · #12E & 28E

Martim Moniz

Largo do Terreirinho · #12E

R. DOS PALMA

CAVALEIROS

R. J. DO OUTEIRO

RUA DE MOURARIA

P. DE COLEGINHO

RUA M. F° DE LIMA

COSTA DO CASTELO

C. DE SANTO ANDRÉ

C. DE GRAÇA

T. DAS MÓNICAS

RUA DAS FARINHAS

CASTELO DE SÃO JORGE

SANTA CRUZ

CASTLE TOWN

MENINO DEUS

MEN DEUS

TELHEIRO

DE SÃO VICENTE

C. DE SÃO VICENTE

SÃO VICENTE DE FORA MONASTERY

R. ESCOLA GERAIS

#2 & 28E

S. CRISTOVÃO

C.M. PANCOS

MARKET

RUA DA MADELENA

RUA DOS FANQUEIROS

DOURADORES

CHÃO DA FERRA

RUA M. S. ANTONIO

RUA DE SÃO MAMEDE

L. LOIOS

S. TIAGO

R. SAUDADE

#12E

R. D. SALVADOR

ESCOLAS

Largo Portas do Sol · #2, 12E & 28E

DEC. ARTS MUSEUM

S. HELENA

Largo Santa Luzia · #2, 12E & 28E

R. D. LIMOEIRO

R. JUDIARIA

S. MIGUEL

S. MIGUEL

R. PEDRO

SÃO ESTEVÃO

RUA REGUEIRA

Largo Chafariz de Dentro

FADO MUSEUM

ALFAMA

To Santa Apolónia & Oriente Train Stations

R. D. C. MOR

R. P. NEGRAS

CRUZES DA SÉ

R. S. ANT°

#2, 12E 15E & 28E

CONCEIÇÃO

S. PADARIA

S. ANTONIO

#2, 12E & 28E

SÉ (CATHEDRAL)

RUA S. J. DA PRAÇA

R. BACALHOEIROS

RUA DA ALFÂNDEGA

R. D. CAIS D. SANTAREM

R. D. TERREIRO TRIGO

R. D. TERREIRO TRIGO

Doca do Terreiro do Trigo

#15E

Praça do Comércio

Terreiro do Paço

Terreiro do Paço

AVENIDA INFANTE DOM HENRIQUE

Doca da Marina

RIVER CRUISES

TERREIRO DO PAÇO FERRY TERMINAL

200 Meters

200 Yards

To Barreiro & Montijo

get info on Lisbon and all of Portugal at the helpful TI (daily 7:00-24:00, tel. 218-450-660). Next to the TI is a handy Vodafone shop that sells Portuguese SIM cards (daily 8:00-22:00).

Getting downtown from Lisbon's very central airport is a snap. There are three options: taxi, shuttle bus, and Metro.

Taxis line up on the curb (if there's a long line, go upstairs to the departure level where, across the street, there's another taxi rank with rarely a line). Rides into town cost about €10. There's a legitimate €1.60 fee for your luggage (not per bag, but to use the trunk). In the past it was tough to get cabbies to use their meter for airport pickups, but these days that rule is more strictly enforced. If the meter starts at €3.90 and is set to *Tarifa 1* (or *Tarifa 2* for nights, weekends, and holidays), relax—you should be fine. There is no "airport fee" supplement. To return to the airport by taxi from downtown to the airport is easy, fast, and cheap. Simply hail one on the street (€10). Skip the €23 taxi vouchers sold by the airport TI—these are for rides outside the center and double your cost.

While dirt-cheap **public buses** leave from the airport curb, these are not really intended for people with luggage. The **AeroBus** is faster and nearly as cheap. You likely want their city center route #1 (€3.50, 3/hour, runs 7:00-23:00, departs outside of arrival level at bus stop marked "AeroBus #1"—not #2), which stops at Marquês de Pombal, Avenida da Liberdade, Restauradores, Rossio, and Praça do Comércio. Route #2 avoids the downtown and ends in the financial district (of no interest to tourists), but makes a handy stop at the bus station at Sete Rios if you plan to go elsewhere immediately (see "By Bus," later). Aerobus tickets are sold at the airport TI or on the bus for the same price.

To take the **Metro**'s red line into Lisbon, exit the airport arrivals hall and turn right to find the Aeroporto stop. Before boarding, buy a reloadable Viva Viagem card at the ticket machine; you can get a 24-hour pass and have Lisbon by the tail for just €6 (see details under "Getting Around Lisbon," later).

By Train

Lisbon has four primary train stations—Santa Apolónia (to Spain and most points north), Oriente (for the Algarve, Évora, and fast trains to the north), Rossio (for Sintra, Óbidos, and Nazaré), and Cais do Sodré (for Cascais and Estoril).

Santa Apolónia Station covers international trains and nearly all of Portugal. Located just east of the Alfama, it has ATMs, a morning-only TI, baggage storage, and good Metro and bus connections to the town center. A taxi from Santa Apolónia Station to any of my recommended hotels costs roughly €8. Bus #794 goes downtown to Praça do Comércio. Bus #759 goes to Rossio and

Praça dos Restauradores. From the station, here's how to get to the bus stop: Look for the Metro sign, walk past the escalators to exit the station, and find the bus stop on your right along busy Avenida Infante Dom Henrique. Most trains using Santa Apolónia Station also stop at **Oriente Station** (Metro: Oriente).

Rossio Station, which handles trains to Sintra (direct, 4/hour, 40 minutes, buy tickets from machines at track level on second floor), is in the town center and an easy walk from most recommended hotels. It also handles trains to Óbidos and Nazaré, but since both destinations require a transfer at Cacém, the bus is a better option. Its all-Portugal ticket office on the ground floor (next to Starbucks) sells long-distance and international train tickets (Mon-Fri 7:00-20:00, closed Sat-Sun, cash only).

Cais do Sodré Station, near the waterfront just west of Praça do Comércio (Metro: Cais do Sodré), serves coastal towns Cascais and Estoril (30 minutes).

By Bus

Lisbon's efficient Sete Rios bus station is in the modern part of the city, several miles inland from the harbor. It has ATMs, a rack of schedules (near entrance), a nifty computer that displays routes and ticket prices, and two information offices—one for buses within Portugal, the other for international routes (Intercentro booth). While you can buy bus tickets up to a week in advance, you can almost always buy a ticket just a few minutes before departure. The EVA company covers the south of Portugal (www.eva-bus.com), while Rede Nacional de Expressos does the rest of the country (www.rede-expressos.pt; bus info for both companies—toll tel. 707-223-344).

The bus station is across the street from the large Sete Rios train station, which sits above the Jardim Zoológico Metro stop. To get from the bus station to downtown Lisbon, it's a €6 taxi ride or a short Metro trip on the blue line (from bus station, walk down and across to Sete Rios train station, then follow signs for *Metro: Jardim Zoológico*).

By Cruise Ship

Lisbon's port is the busiest on Europe's Atlantic coast, with most cruise ships docking at one of two terminals: Alcântara (about two miles west of downtown) or Santa Apolónia (near the train station of the same name, at the base of the Alfama).

Both terminals have ATMs, and WCs, public phones, and taxi stands. The taxis that wait at either terminal are notoriously dishonest. For a fair, metered rate, you might have better luck walking across the big street and hailing one as it drives by. Even better, choose among the following options:

Most cruise lines offer inexpensive shuttle service from either terminal to Praça do Comércio. If you're taking public transit from the Alcântara terminal, you can reach central Lisbon on trolley #15E (use pedestrian underpass to reach trolley stop, 5/hour, 15 minutes, €3, coins only) or on any bus (direction: Centro, €2, pay the driver). From the Santa Apolónia cruise-ship terminal, it's a short walk to the Santa Apolónia train station, described earlier under "By Train." From this terminal, bus #794 goes to Praça do Comércio. Transfer there via trolley #15E or bus #714 out to Belém.

By Car

It makes absolutely no sense to drive in Lisbon. If you're starting your trip in Lisbon, don't rent a car until you're on your way out of town.

If you enter Lisbon from the north, a series of boulevards takes you into the center. Navigate by following signs to *Centro, Avenida da República, Marquês de Pombal, Avenida da Liberdade, Praça dos Restauradores, Rossio,* and *Praça do Comércio.* If coming from the east over the Vasco da Gama Bridge and heading for the airport, take the first exit after the bridge.

If you're turning in your car in Lisbon, consider dropping it at the airport (rental-car turn-in clearly signposted, no extra expense to drop it here, very helpful TI open late) and riding a sweat-free taxi for €10 to your hotel. Or, if you must drive into town, consider hiring a taxi and following it to your hotel.

There are many safe underground pay parking lots in Lisbon (follow blue *P* signs), but they discourage anything but short stays by getting more expensive by the hour. They can cost a maximum €20 per day (at the most central Praça dos Restauradores).

HELPFUL HINTS

Theft Alert: Lisbon has piles of people doing illegal business on the street. While the city is generally safe, if you're looking for trouble—especially after dark—you may find it. Pickpockets target tourists on the trolleys (especially #12E, #15E, and #28E) and on the Metro.

Enjoy the sightseeing, but seriously be aware of your surroundings—wear your money belt and keep your pack zipped up. Many thieves pose as tourists by wearing cameras and toting maps. Be on guard whenever you're in a crush of people, or jostled as you enter or leave a tram or bus. If you carry valuables in your pockets, keep your hands on them when possible.

You'll see Gypsies begging on the street—some are scammers and pickpockets. They're generally Romanians who, with that country's membership in the European Union, are free to roam and take advantage of Europe's generous social security. Portugal has its poor, but they are generally too proud to work the system and are considered "the invisible poor."

Pedestrian Warning: Sidewalks can be narrow in certain neighborhoods, and drivers are daring; cross the street with care. The cobbles, while picturesque, can be very slippery. And trams can sneak up on you if you're not paying attention.

Calendar Concerns: National museums are free on Sunday (all day or until 14:00). Many major sights are closed on Monday, including Lisbon's Gulbenkian Museum, Museum of Ancient Art, National Tile Museum, and Fado Museum, as well as Belém's Monastery of Jerónimos, Coach Museum, and Belém Tower. Tuesdays and Saturdays are flea- and food-market days in the Alfama's Campo de Santa Clara. Bullfights take place irregularly throughout the summer, mainly on Thursdays.

Laundry: Drop off clothes at centrally located **5àSec Lavandaria** (€7.50/kilo, same-day wash-and-dry service, Mon-Fri 8:00-20:00, Sat-Sun 10:00-20:00, near Baixa-Chiado Metro stop at Rua do Crucifixo 99, tel. 213-479-599). Hostels and shopping malls generally have laundry services, or your hotelier can recommend a place nearby.

Internet Access: Praça da Figueira has downtown's most convenient Internet café (**Western Union,** on corner nearest the Church of São Domingos, Mon-Fri 8:15-20:15, Sat-Sun 9:00-19:15, longer hours in summer, €1.25/30 minutes). There are other cheap hole-in-the-wall shops catering to immigrants' need for low-cost Internet access.

Post Office and Telephones: The post offices *(correios)* at Praça dos Restauradores 58 (Mon-Fri 8:00-22:00, Sat 9:00-18:00) and on Rua da Santa Justa 15 (Mon-Fri 9:00-18:00) are modern and user-friendly. The **Western Union** office mentioned above in "Internet Access" also has metered phones.

Travel Agency: Agencies line the Avenida da Liberdade. For flights (and train tickets in Portugal only—same price as at station, no fee), **GeoStar** is handy and helpful (€15 booking fee for flights, Mon-Fri 9:30-18:30, closed Sat-Sun, Praça dos Restauradores 14, tel. 213-245-240).

Ticket Kiosk: The green **ABEP kiosk** at the bottom end of Praça dos Restauradores is a handy spot to buy a city transit pass, LisboaCard, and tickets to just about anything: bullfights, soccer games, concerts, and other events. They know what's on (daily 9:00-20:00, across from TI).

Updates to This Book: For updates to this book, check www.ricksteves.com/update.

GETTING AROUND LISBON

To use Lisbon's transit economically, either use your LisboaCard or take advantage of the reloadable Viva Viagem card (a paper card containing a magnetic strip). The card works on the Metro, funiculars, trolleys, buses, and some trains.

Viva Viagem cards are sold at smart machines at any Metro stop for a one-time €0.50 fee and loaded with your choice of options: single ride (€1.40, good for one hour of travel within Zone 1); 24-hour pass (€6, not valid for trains); or "Zapping" (pre-load the card with up to €15, and credit is deducted at the single-ride rate of €1.40 as you use it—you can "top it up" when the credit runs out; valid on trains). For intense users, the 24-hour pass is best. If using the system more sparingly, "Zapping" is better (www.carris. pt). Note, too, that the 24-hour pass cannot be used for trains, but "Zapping" cards can get you to Sintra, Cascais, or Estorial by train with no problem.

To buy or top up your Viva Viagem card at a smart machine, touch the screen to begin, press the British flag for English, then make your selection: "without a reusable card" for first-time users, or "with a reusable card" to top up. To buy a card without using the machine—or to get information on the system—drop by the Casa da Sorte office (see blue sign from Rossio and Praça da Figueira, Mon-Fri 8:00-20:00, closed Sat-Sun).

Hang onto your Viva Viagem card, as you'll need to place it on the magnetic pad when entering and leaving the system, and to avoid paying an extra €0.50 each time you buy a ticket.

By Metro

Lisbon's simple, fast, and color-coded subway system is a delight to use (runs daily 6:30-1:00 in the morning). Though it's not necessary for getting around the historic downtown, the Metro is handy for trips to or from Rossio (Metro: Rossio or Restauradores), Praça do Comércio (Metro: Terreiro do Paço), the Gulbenkian Museum (Metro: São Sebastião), the

Chiado neighborhood (Metro: Baixa-Chiado), Centro Colombo shopping mall (Metro: Colégio Militar/Luz), Parque das Nações and the Oriente train station (both at Metro: Oriente), Sete Rios

bus and train stations (Metro: Jardim Zoológico), and the airport (Metro: Aeroporto).

With the Viva Viagem card (described earlier), a Metro ride costs €1.40 within Zone 1 (which includes everything of interest to most tourists). Place the card flat on the magnetic scanner as you enter, and keep the card handy until your trip is over—you'll need it again to exit the sliding doors.

Metro stops are marked above ground with a red "M." *Saída* means exit. You can find a Metro map at any Metro stop, on most city maps, and on the Metro website (www.metrolisboa.pt/eng/).

By Trolley, Funicular, and Bus

Lisbon's buses are fine, but for fun and practical public transportation, use the trolleys and funiculars. Buy your ticket from the driver (bus-€2, trolley-€3, no transfers), or use your Viva Viagem card (€1.40/ride if "Zapping" or covered by €6 24-hour pass). Like San Francisco, Lisbon sees its trolleys as part of its heritage, and has kept a few in use. Trolleys #12E (circling the Alfama) and #28E (a scenic ride across the old town) use vintage cars; #15E (to Belém) uses a modern version. Buy a ticket, have a pass, or risk a big fine on the spot. Please be mindful of locals—especially little old Alfama ladies—who need a seat. Funiculars cost €3.60 round-trip if you don't have a pass. Also see "Trolley" under "Tours in Lisbon," later.

By Taxi

Lisbon is a great taxi town. Cabbies are good-humored and (except for crooked ones at the cruise terminals) willing to use their meters. Rides start at €3.90, and you can go anywhere in the center for around €6. Decals on the window clearly spell out all charges in English. The meter should start at €3.90 and be set to *Tarifa 1* (Mon-Fri 6:00-21:00, including the airport) or *Tarifa 2* (same drop rate, a little more per kilometer; for nights, weekends, and holidays). If the meter reads *Tarifa 3, 4,* or *5,* simply ask the cabbie to change it, unless you're going to Belém, which is considered outside the city limits of Lisbon.

Cabs are generally easy to hail on the street (green light means available, lit number on the roof indicates it's taken). If you're having a hard time flagging one down, ask a passerby for the location of the nearest taxi stand: *praça de taxi* (PRAH-sah duh taxi). They're all over the town center.

Especially if you're with a companion, Lisbon's cabs are a cheap time-saver. For an average trip, couples save only a few dollars each by taking public transportation, but spend an extra 15 minutes getting there—bad economics. If you're traveling with a companion and your time is limited, taxi everywhere.

LISBON

LISBON

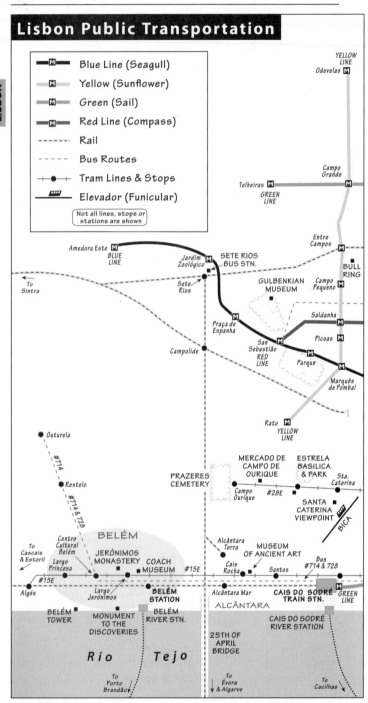

Lisbon Public Transportation

- ━M━ Blue Line (Seagull)
- ━M━ Yellow (Sunflower)
- ━M━ Green (Sail)
- ━M━ Red Line (Compass)
- ········· Rail
- ----- Bus Routes
- +●+ Tram Lines & Stops
- ▱ Elevador (Funicular)

Not all lines, stops or stations are shown

YELLOW LINE
Odevelas M

Campo Grande M

Telheiras M
GREEN LINE

Entre Campos M

Amedora Este M
BLUE LINE

Jardim Zoológico
SETE RIOS BUS STN.

Sete Rios

To Sintra

GULBENKIAN MUSEUM
Campo Pequeno M
BULL RING

Praça de Espanha

Saldanha

Campolide

San Sebastião
RED LINE M

Picoas M

Parque

Marquês de Pombal M

Rato M
YELLOW LINE

Outurela

#714

Restelo

#714 & 728

PRAZERES CEMETERY

MERCADO DE CAMPO DE OURIQUE

ESTRELA BASILICA & PARK

Sta. Caterina

Campo Ourique
#28E

SANTA CATERINA VIEWPOINT

BICA

To Cascais & Estoril

Centro Cultural Belém

BELÉM

JERÓNIMOS MONASTERY

Alcântara Terra

MUSEUM OF ANCIENT ART

Largo Princesa

COACH MUSEUM
#15E

Cais Rocha

Santos

Bus #714 & 728

#15E

Algés

Largo Jerónimos

BELÉM STATION

Alcântara Mar

CAIS DO SODRÉ TRAIN STN.

GREEN LINE M

BELÉM TOWER

MONUMENT TO THE DISCOVERIES

BELÉM RIVER STN.

ALCÂNTARA

CAIS DO SODRÉ RIVER STATION

25TH OF APRIL BRIDGE

Rio   Tejo

To Porto Brandão

To Évora & Algarve

To Cacilhas

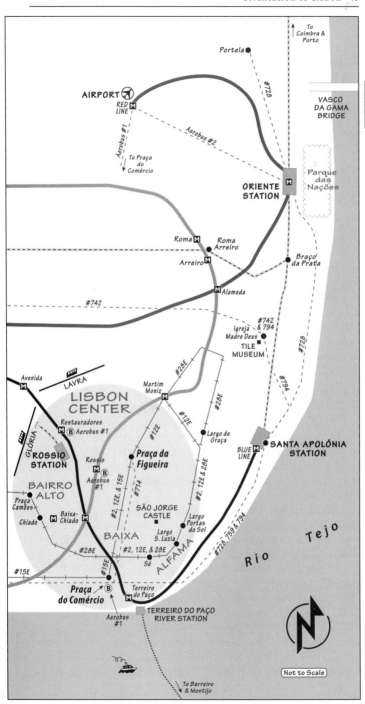

Tours in Lisbon

ON WHEELS
▲▲Trolleys

Lisbon's trolleys, many vintage models from the 1920s, shake and shiver through the old parts of town, somehow safely weaving

within inches of parked cars, climbing steep hills, and offering sightseers breezy views of the city (rubberneck out the window and you die). As you board, pay the driver (€3) or swipe your Viva Viagem card (much cheaper), take a seat, and watch the pensioners as they lurch by. Buses and trolleys usually share the same stops and routes. Signs for bus stops list the bus number, while signs for trolley stops include an E (for *eléctrico*) before or after the route number. Remember that most pickpocketing in Lisbon takes place on trolleys, so enjoy the ride, but keep an eye on your belongings. You can think of trolleys #28E and #12E as hop-on, hop-off do-it-yourself tours ("Zapping" tickets are good for an hour, and with a 24-hour pass, hopping on and off is essentially free).

Trolley #28E

Trolley #28E is a San Francisco-style Lisbon joyride. In the center of town, this trolley is often extremely crowded. To enjoy a seat for the entire scenic ride, consider taking a taxi to Mercado de Campo de Ourique for a meal or to the Prazeres Cemetery (both described next) and catching the #28E from there, where it starts its route across town. The following are notable trolley stops from west to east:

The Prazeres Cemetery, at the western terminus of route #28E, is a vast park-like necropolis dense with the mausoleums of leading Lisbon families and historic figures dating back to the 19th century (daily 9:00-17:00).

Mercado de Campo de Ourique, at the first stop after the Prazeres Cemetery (stop: Igreja Sto. Condestáovel), is a 19th-century iron-and-glass market that's now a trendy food circus (daily 10:00-23:00). The market is behind the big church on Campo de Ourique.

At the **Estrela Basilica and Park,** you'll see the 18th-century, late Baroque basilica, with stairs winding up to the roof for a view both out and down into the church (for €4), and across the street,

Lisbon's Best Viewpoints
(*Miradouros* and *Belvederes*)

The first three viewpoints are included in the self-guided walks described in this chapter:

- Miradouro de São Pedro de Alcântara (view terrace in Bairro Alto, at top of Elevador da Glória funicular; see "The Bairro Alto and Chiado Stroll," page 41)
- São Jorge Castle (on top of the Alfama; see photo above and "The Alfama Stroll and the Castle," page 23)
- Miradouro de Largo das Portas do Sol (south slope of Alfama; see "The Alfama Stroll and the Castle," page 23)
- Elevador de Santa Justa (in the Baixa, page 46)
- Cristo Rei (statue on hillside across the Rio Tejo, page 63)
- Edward VII Park (at north end of Avenida da Liberdade)
- Bica Miradouro (atop the Elevador da Bica funicular)

the Estrela Park—a cozy neighborhood scene with pond-side café and a "garden library kiosk."

Bica is great for a stroll through the characteristic back side of the Bairro Alto over to the Miradouro de Santa Catarina (a great view terrace with inviting cafés and bars) and the top of the Elevador da Bica funicular (which drops steeply through a rough-and-tumble neighborhood to the riverfront).

Trolley #28E then laces together **Chiado** (at Chiado's main square, Lisbon's café and "Latin Quarter"); **Baixa** (on Rua da Conceição between Augusta and Prata); **Sé** (the cathedral); **Miradouro de Largo das Portas do Sol** (the Alfama viewpoint); **Campo de Santa Clara** (flea market on Tue and Sat); and the pleasant and untouristy **Graça** district (with another excellent viewpoint).

Trolley #12E

For a colorful, 20-minute loop around the castle and the Alfama, catch trolley #12E on Praça da Figueira (departs every few minutes from the stop at corner of square closest to castle). The driver can tell you when to get out for the Miradouro de Largo das Portas do Sol (viewpoint) near the castle (about three-quarters of the way up the hill), or stay on the trolley and you'll be dropped back where you started. Here's what you'll see on this loop ride:

Leaving Praça da Figueira, you enter **Largo de Martim Moniz**—named for a knight who died heroically while using his body as a doorjamb to leave the castle gate open, allowing his Christian Portuguese comrades to get in and capture Lisbon from the Moors in 1147. On the right is the picturesque Centro Comercial da Mouraria, a **marketplace** filled with a wide variety of products and aromas from around the world. The big, maroon-colored building capping the hill on the left was a Jesuit monastery until 1769, when the dictatorial Marquês de Pombal booted the pesky order out of Portugal and turned the building into the Hospital São Jose. Today, this is an immigrant neighborhood with lots of cheap import shops.

Turning right onto Rua de Cavaleiros, you climb through the atmospheric **Mouraria neighborhood** on a street so narrow that a single trolley track is all that fits. Notice how the colorful mix of neighbors who fill the trolley all seem to know each other. If the trolley's path is blocked and can't pass, lots of horn-honking and shouts from passengers ensue until your journey resumes. Look up the skinny side streets. Marvel at the creative parking and classic laundry scenes. This was the area given to the Moors after they were driven out of the castle and Alfama. Natives know it as the home of the legendary fado singer Maria Severa as well as modern-day singer Mariza. The majority of residents these days are immigrants from Asia, making this Lisbon's version of Chinatown and Bollywood wrapped up in one.

At the crest of the hill **(Largo Rodrigues de Freitas),** you can get out to explore, eat at a cheap restaurant (see "Eating in Lisbon," later), or follow Rua de Santa Marinha to the Campo de Santa Clara flea market (Tue and Sat).

When you see the river, you're at **Largo das Portas do Sol** (Gates of the Sun), where you'll also see the remains of one of the seven old Moorish gates of Lisbon. The driver usually announces *"castelo"* (cahzh-TAY-loo) at this point. Hop out here if you want to visit the Museum and School of Portuguese Decorative Arts, enjoy the most scenic cup of coffee in town, explore the **Alfama,** or tour the **castle.**

The trolley continues downhill past the fortress-like **cathedral** (Sé, on left) and into the **Baixa** (grid-planned Pombaline city). After a few blocks, you're back where you started—Praça da Figueira.

Trolley #2

A new hop-on, hop-off "tourist trolley," using green vintage cars marked "Lisbon Historical Route/Castle Line," runs from **Praça da Figueira** through the **Baixa,** past the **cathedral** (Sé), into the **Alfama** past **Miradouro de Largo das Portas do Sol** (the Alfama viewpoint), and up to **Largo da Graça,** where the line ends (€9 ticket valid for 24 hours, not covered by Viva Viagem cards, runs 10:00-17:40, 40 minutes, with audio commentary in English, Portuguese, and French).

By Bus and Tram

Yellow Bus Tours

Yellow Bus Tours offers three different downtown tours (all hop-on, hop-off). While uninspiring and not cheap, they're handy and run daily year-round. The tram and bus tours, which last about 1.5 hours, start and end at Praça da Figueira (look for yellow bus and tram signs at stops, buy tickets from driver). For more info, stop by the TI at Praça do Comércio or Praça dos Restauradores, or contact Yellow Bus (tel. 213-478-030, www.yellowbustours.com). Tickets for their hop-on, hop-off tours do double-duty as a 24-hour public transit pass, covering Lisbon's trolleys, buses, Elevador de Santa Justa, and funiculars (but not the Metro, which is owned by a different company).

Hop-on, Hop-off Bus Tours

Two tours on yellow, double-decker buses make overlapping loops around Lisbon, starting from Praça da Figueira (€15 apiece, includes audioguide). You can get off, tour a sight, and catch a later bus. The **Tagus Tour** covers north and west Lisbon, stopping at major sights such as the Museum of Ancient Art and Belém (runs every 15 minutes June-Sept 9:00-20:00, fewer in winter). The **Olisipo Tour** covers east Lisbon, with stops at Parque das Nações, the National Tile Museum, and more (runs every 30 minutes year-round 9:15-19:15, shorter hours in winter). You cannot hop on and hop off between the two different tours without buying a second ticket. You can combine a Tagus Tour with the Cruzeiros no Tejo boat tour (see "By Boat," later) for a discount.

Hills Tramcar Tour

This hop-on, hop-off tour takes you on a shiny red 1900s tramcar through the Alfama, Bairro Alto, and other Lisbon hills (€18, 1.5-hour tour with five stops, recorded narration available in English, runs every 20 minutes June-Sept 9:15-19:00, fewer off-season).

Gray Line/Cityrama Tours

Another option for hop-on, hop-off tours, the red Gray Line/Cityrama buses, offer four routes: The **Castle** line covers the Alfama and city center; the **Belém** line gets you to that district; the **Oriente** line includes Bairro Alto and Parque das Nações; and the **Cascais** line heads west along the coast past the charming beach towns of Estoril and Cascais to the scenic beaches near Guincho. Buses have free onboard Wi-Fi, making multitasking a snap (one line–€12, two lines–€18, four lines–€25, one-line ticket valid 24 hours, multi-line tickets valid 48 hours, recorded English narration available; Castle and Belém lines run 2/hour April-Oct 9:30-18:00, Oriente line runs every 45 minutes, Cascais line departs 6/day but last bus doesn't return to Lisbon).

The main info kiosk is at the north side of Marquês de Pombal roundabout, but you can purchase tickets at any TI or on board (tel. 800-208-513, www.cityrama.pt). Tickets also include discounts to certain sights.

BY BOAT
Rio Tejo Cruise
Cruzeiros no Tejo runs two river tour routes. Their longer tour does a big east-west loop to the Vasco da Gama Bridge and Parque das Nações, then to Belém and back (€20, daily at 15:00, 2.5 hours, departs from Terreiro do Paço dock off Praça do Comércio). Their shorter tour makes a loop downtown to Belém and back (€15, departs from Terreiro do Paço at 11:15, same boat departs from Cais do Sodré ferry terminal at 11:30, also an afternoon departure from Cais do Sodré at 16:15). Each operates April through October and comes with a four-language narration (free drinks and WC on board, tel. 210-422-417, www.transtejo.pt). An interesting way to visit Belém would be to take the 11:00 boat from either downtown terminal, see the Monastery of Jerónimos and related sights, then return in the afternoon from the Belém ferry terminal (departures approximately at 16:45, confirm hours when purchasing tickets).

Another outfit, **Lisboa Vista do Tejo,** runs tours from Cais do Sodré to the Belém Tower (at 11:45 and 15:15) and vice versa (at 14:00 and 16:30). Trips are narrated in Portuguese and English (€12 one-way, €16 round-trip, April-Oct, no Mon tours, one hour each way, book ahead, tel. 213-913-030, www.lvt.pt).

Cheap River Ferry Ride to Cacilhas
For a quick, cheap trip across the river with great city and bridge views in the company of Lisbon commuters rather than tourists, hop the ferry to Cacilhas (kah-SEE-lahsh) from the Cais do Sodré Station (a 10-minute walk from Praça do Comércio). At the terminal, follow signs to *Cacilhas*, not *Montijo* (€1.20 each way, 4/hour weekdays, fewer on weekends, signs say *partida*—departure—and *destino*). Either hop out for a look at the rough little industrial port, or stay on for a 25-minute round-trip.

Ways to Get from the Baixa Up to the Bairro Alto and Chiado

- Ride the Elevador da Glória funicular (a few blocks north of Rossio on Avenida da Liberdade, opposite the Hard Rock Café), or hike alongside the tracks if the funicular isn't running.
- Walk up lots of stairs from Rossio (due west of the central column).
- Taxi to the Miradouro de São Pedro de Alcântara.
- Take the escalator at the Baixa-Chiado Metro stop.
- Catch trolley #28E from Rua da Conceição.
- Hike up Rua do Carmo from Rossio to Rua Garrett.
- Take escalators or elevators from the Armazéns mall to Rua Garrett.
- Take the Elevador de Santa Justa, which goes right by the Convento do Carmo and the Chiado.

ON FOOT
Walking Tours

Two walking-tour companies—Lisbon Walker and Inside Lisbon—offer excellent, affordable tours led by young, top-notch guides with a passion for sharing insights to their hometown. Well-priced to start with, both companies give my readers their discounted student prices. Tour groups are small (generally 2-12 people) and given in English only. Each company has a helpful website explaining their tours and has an easygoing style. With either company, you'll likely feel you've made a friend in your guide (a great way to get to know a local). Especially with the substantial discount given to readers of this book, these tours are time and money very well spent.

Lisbon Walker

Standard tours include: "Revelation" (best 3-hour overview with good coverage of the Baixa and the main squares, a quick look at the Bairro Alto, and a trolley ride across town to the Graça viewpoint); "Old Town" (2-hour walk through Alfama that examines the origins of Lisbon—Romans, Moors, and its castle); and "Downtown" (2-3 hours, covers the 1755 earthquake and the rebirth of Lisbon). Other more-focused tours are "Legends & Mysteries," "City of Spies," and "Castle Hill," which includes the tangled, multi-ethnic Mouraria neighborhood (€15/person; €10 for youth, seniors, and those with this book; daily year-round at 10:00, meet at northwest corner of Praça do Comércio near Rua do Arsenal, in front of the TI—tel. 218-861-840, www.lisbonwalker.com).

Inside Lisbon

Tours include the "Best of Lisbon Walk" (a good highlights tour of the main squares, the Chiado, and the Alfama; €18, daily year-round at 10:00) and food and wine tours (see "Food Tours," next). Most tours meet at the statue of Dom Pedro IV in the center of Rossio and last about three to four hours. A €5 discount is offered to anyone with this book (reserve by the day before the tour via website or phone, tel. 968-412-612, www.insidelisbon.com). They also offer private tours and day trips by minivan to Sintra/Cascais and Obidos/Fátima. You can organize a private city tour with them, or use their helpful website as a resource for seeing Lisbon on your own.

Food Tours

Guided food tours are trendy these days. Several companies offer three- to four-hour multi-stop tours that introduce you to lots of local food culture while filling your stomach at the same time (search the Web for the latest).

I've enjoyed tours by several good outfits. In each case, the groups are small, the teaching is great, and—when you figure into it the cost of the meal—the tours are a solid value.

Inside Lisbon offers a €35 "Food and Wine Walk," which makes five to six short, tasty, and memorable stand-up stops, as well as a €35 "Lisbon Experience Walk," a walking-and-eating tour from Praça dos Restauradores to Mouraria, ending with a ferry to Cacilhas for seafood (www.insidelisbon.com).

Two different companies, **Eat Portugal** and **Eat Drink Walk,** offer similar slower-paced, more top-end, and substantial tours. Their €66 tapas walks have five to six stops, and their €85 gourmet walks stop at finer places, with lots of food and local wines (www.eatportugal.com, Celia; www.eatdrinkwalk.com, Filomena).

Local Guides

Hiring a private local guide in Lisbon can be a wonderful luxury. They'll meet you at your hotel and tailor a tour to your interests. Especially with a small group, this can be a fine value. Audioguides are rare in Lisbon, so having your own guide can really help. Guides charge roughly the same rates (Mon-Fri €100-125/half-day, €195/day). Delightful **Alex Almeida** runs **Your Friend in Lisbon** tours (mobile 919-292-151, alex@yourfriendinlisbon.com). **Cristina Duarte** leads tours for my company and knows Lisbon well (mobile 919-316-242, acrismduarte@gmail.com). **Claudia da Costa,** whom you may have seen on my Lisbon TV show, is also excellent (mobile 965-560-216, claudiadacosta@hotmail.com).

Cristina Quental is another fine local guide (mobile 919-922-480, anacristinaquental@hotmail.com).

The "Three Neighborhoods" Walk

The essential Lisbon is easily and enjoyably covered in three self-guided walking tours (described next). You can explore Lisbon's three downtown neighborhoods—the Alfama, Baixa, and Bairro Alto—either as individual walks or by lacing them together into a single walk (which would take a minimum of five hours, but could be done as a more leisurely all-day experience). While it's easy to do these walks in any order you like, starting with the Alfama lets you get to the castle before the crowds hit (avoiding the need to line up for a ticket) and kick things off with the grand city view from Lisbon's fortified birthplace. Doing the walks in this order makes connecting them convenient as well. And you'll finish in the liveliest quarter for evening fun—the Bairro Alto/Chiado.

▲▲▲THE ALFAMA STROLL AND THE CASTLE

Explore the Alfama, the colorful sailors' quarter that dates back to the age of Visigoth occupation, from the sixth to eighth centuries A.D. This was a bustling district during the Moorish period, and eventually became the home of Lisbon's fishermen and mariners (and of the poet Luís de Camões, who wrote, "Our lips meet easily, high across the narrow street"). The Alfama's tangled street plan is one of the few features of Lisbon to survive the 1755 earthquake. It helps make the neighborhood a cobbled playground of Old World color. Visit at the best time, during the busy mid-morning market, or in the cooler hours in the late afternoon or early evening, when the streets teem with residents. While much of its grittiness has been cleaned up in recent years (as traditional residents have been replaced by immigrant laborers), the Alfama remains one of Europe's most photogenic neighborhoods.

• *Start your walk at the highest point in town, São Jorge Castle. Get to the castle gate by taxi (€5) or by minibus #737 from Praça da Figueira. (Trolleys #28E and #12E go to Largo Santa Luzia and Largo das Portas do Sol, respectively, a few blocks below.)*

❶ São Jorge Castle Gate and Fortified Castle Town

The formidable gate to the castle is part of a fortification that, these days, surrounds three things: the view terrace, the small town that stood within the walls, and the castle itself. The ticket office is in the small town, and the turnstile is situated so that those without a ticket are kept away from the view terrace and castle proper (castle entry-€7.50, daily March-Oct 9:00-21:00, Nov-Feb 9:00-18:00).

Just inside the castle gate (on left) is a little statue of George,

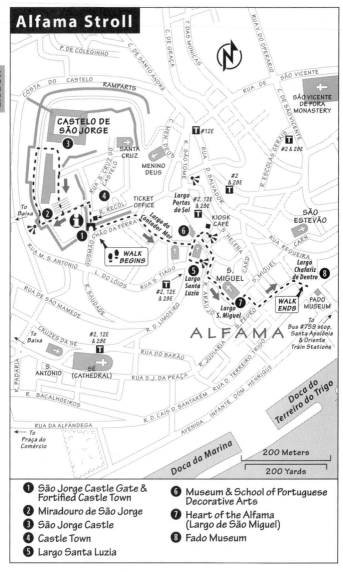

Alfama Stroll

- ① São Jorge Castle Gate & Fortified Castle Town
- ② Miradouro de São Jorge
- ③ São Jorge Castle
- ④ Castle Town
- ⑤ Largo Santa Luzia
- ⑥ Museum & School of Portuguese Decorative Arts
- ⑦ Heart of the Alfama (Largo de São Miguel)
- ⑧ Fado Museum

named for a popular saint in the 14th century. St. George (São Jorge; pronounced "sow ZHOR-zh") hailed from Turkey and was known for fighting valiantly (he's often portrayed slaying a dragon). When the Christian noble Afonso Henriques called for help to eliminate the Moors from his newly founded country of Portugal, the Crusaders who helped him prayed to St. George... and won.

LISBON

(If money is tight, the castle and view are skippable—the castle is just stark, rebuilt ruins from the Salazar era, and while the hill-capping park has a commanding view, there are other fine views coming up...just jump ahead to stop #4 on this walk.)

• *If you decide to go in, pick up your ticket and then follow the cobbles uphill past the first lanes of old Lisbon into the Miradouro de São Jorge.*

❷ Miradouro de São Jorge (View Terrace)

Enjoy the grand view. The Rio Tejo is one of five main rivers in Portugal, four of which come from Spain. (Only the Mondego River, which passes by Coimbra, originates inside Portuguese territory, in the Serra de Estrela.) While Portugal and Spain generally have very good relations, a major sore point is the control of all this water. From here, you have a good view of the 25th of April Bridge, which leads south to the Cristo Rei statue. Past the bridge, you can barely see the Monument to the Discoveries and the Belém Tower on a clear day.

Look up at the statue marking the center of this terrace. Afonso Henriques, a warlord with a strong personal army, was the founder of Portugal. In 1147 he besieged this former Moorish castle until the hungry, thirsty residents gave in. Every Portuguese schoolkid knows the story of this man—a Reconquista hero and their country's first king.

Stroll inland along the **ramparts** for a more extensive view of Pombal's Lisbon, described in a circa-1963 tile-panorama chart (which lacks the big 25th of April Bridge—it was built in 1969). From Praça do Comércio on the water, the grid streets of the Baixa lead up to the tree-lined Avenida da Liberdade and the big Edward VII Park, often capped with a large Portuguese flag on the far right. Locate city landmarks, such as the Elevador de Santa Justa (the Eiffel-style elevator in front of the ruined Convento do Carmo) and the sloping white roof of Rossio Station.

After walking farther inland under the second arch, take a right and then a left to wander the grounds. Then enter the inner castle (which usually only offers a chance to climb up for more views). The strolling peacocks remind visitors that exotic birds like these came to Lisbon originally as trophies of the great 16th-century voyages and discoveries.

❸ São Jorge Castle

While the first settlements here go back to the 7th century B.C., this castle dates to the 11th century when Moors built it to house their army and provide a safe haven where their elites could retreat

Lisbon at a Glance

In Lisbon

▲▲▲**Alfama Stroll and the Castle** Tangled medieval streets topped by São Jorge Castle. See page 23.

▲▲▲**Baixa Stroll: Lisbon's Historic Downtown** The lower town, gridded with streets and dotted with major squares. See page 32.

▲▲▲**Bairro Alto and Chiado Stroll** The high town's views, churches, and Chiado fashion district. See page 41.

▲▲▲**Gulbenkian Museum** Lisbon's best museum, featuring an art collection spanning 5,000 years, from ancient Egyptian to Impressionist to Art Nouveau. **Hours:** Tue-Sun 10:00-18:00, closed Mon. See page 51.

▲▲**Museum of Ancient Art** Portuguese paintings from the 15th- and 16th-century glory days. **Hours:** Tue 14:00-18:00, Wed-Sun 10:00-18:00, closed Mon. See page 55.

▲▲**Parque das Nações** Inviting waterfront park with a long promenade (and rental bikes), modern mall, aquarium, and the Expo '98 fairgrounds. **Hours:** Park always open. See page 57.

▲**Fado Museum** The story of Portuguese folk music. **Hours:** Tue-Sun 10:00-18:00, closed Mon. See page 32.

▲**National Tile Museum** Tons of artistic tiles, including a panorama of pre-earthquake Lisbon. **Hours:** Tue-Sun 10:00-18:00, closed Mon. See page 61.

▲**São Roque Church and Museum** Fine 16th-century Jesuit church with false dome ceiling, chapel made of precious stones, and a less-interesting museum. **Hours:** Tue-Sun 9:00-18:00, Mon 14:00-18:00. See page 44.

Port Wine Institute Plush place selling tastes of the world's greatest selection of ports. **Hours:** Mon-Sat 11:00-24:00, closed Sun. See page 42.

São Jorge Castle Originally an eighth-century bastion, first built by the Moors, with kingly views at the highest point in town.

Hours: Daily March-Oct 9:00-21:00, Nov-Feb 9:00-18:00. See page 25.

Museum and School of Portuguese Decorative Arts A stroll through aristocratic households richly decorated in 16th- to 19th-century styles. **Hours:** Wed-Mon 10:00-17:00, closed Tue. See page 30.

Elevador de Santa Justa A 150-foot-tall iron elevator offering a glittering city vista. **Hours:** Daily 7:00-21:30. See page 46.

Cathedral (Sé) From the outside, an impressive Romanesque fortress of God; inside, not much. **Hours:** Church—daily Tue-Sat 9:00-19:00, Sun-Mon 9:00-17:00; cloister—Tue-Sat 10:00-18:30, Mon 10:00-17:00, closed Sun. See page 50.

In Belém

Note that all of these sights—except the Monument to the Discoveries—are closed on Monday year-round.

▲▲▲**Monastery of Jerónimos** King Manuel's giant 16th-century, white limestone church and monastery, with remarkable cloister and the explorer Vasco da Gama's tomb. **Hours:** May-Sept Tue-Sun 10:00-18:30, off-season until 17:30, closed Mon. See page 67.

▲▲**National Coach Museum** Dozens of carriages, from simple to opulent, displaying the evolution of coaches from 1600 on. **Hours:** Tue-Sun 10:00-18:00, closed Mon. See page 66.

▲**Maritime Museum** A salty selection of exhibits on the ships and navigational tools of the Age of Discovery. **Hours:** May-Sept daily 10:00-18:00, off-season until 17:00. See page 72.

▲**Monument to the Discoveries** Giant riverside monument honoring the explorers who brought Portugal great power and riches centuries ago. **Hours:** May-Sept daily 10:00-19:00; Oct-April Tue-Sun 10:00-18:00, closed Mon. See page 73.

▲**Belém Tower** Consummate Manueline building with a worthwhile view up 120 steps. **Hours:** May-Sept Tue-Sun 10:00-18:30, off-season until 17:30, closed Mon. See page 76.

in times of siege. After Afonso Henriques took the castle in 1147, Portugal's royalty lived here for several centuries. The sloping walls—typical of castles from this period—were designed to withstand 14th-century cannonballs. In the 16th century, the kings moved to their palace on Praça do Comércio and the castle became

a military garrison. Despite suffering major damage in the 1755 earthquake, the castle later served another stint as a military garrison. In the 20th century, it became a national monument.

As you explore the castle's inner sanctum, imagine it lined with simple wooden huts. The imposing part of the castle is the exterior. The builders' strategy was to focus on making the castle appear so formidable that its very existence was enough to discourage any attack. If you know where to look, you can still see stones laid by ancient Romans, Visigoths, and Moors. The Portuguese made the most substantial contribution, with a wall reaching all the way to the river to withstand anticipated Spanish attacks.

The humble museum (between the castle and the view terrace) houses archaeological finds from the 7th century B.C. to the 18th century, with emphasis on the Moorish period in the 11th and 12th centuries. You'll also see 18th-century tiles from an age when Portugal was flush with money from its colony, Brazil. While simple, the museum has nice displays and descriptions.

❹ Castle Town

Just outside the castle turnstile is the tiny neighborhood within the castle walls built to give Moorish elites refuge from sieges and, later, for Portuguese nobles to live close to their king. While it's partly taken over by cute shops and cafés, if you wander up Rua de Santa Cruz do Castelo and stroll into its back lanes, you can enjoy a peaceful bit of Portugal's past. Most of the houses date from the Middle Ages. Poking around, go on a cultural scavenger hunt. Look for: 1) clever, space-efficient, triangular contraptions for drying clothes (hint: see the bottle cap in the wall used to prop the sticks out when in use); 2) Benfica soccer team flag (that's the team favored by Lisbon's working class—an indication that the upper class no longer chooses to live here); 3) short doors that were tall enough for people back when these houses were built; and 4) noble family crests over doors—dating to when important families wanted to be close to the king.

• *Leave the castle. Across the ramp from the castle entrance (just outside the turnstile 20 yards ahead, on the left) is a tidy little castle district with cute shops and cafés, worth a wander for its peaceful lanes and a*

Pombal's Lisbon

In 1750, lazy King José I (r. 1750-1777) turned the government over to a minor noble, the Marquês de Pombal (1699-1782). Talented, ambitious, and handsome, Pombal was praised as a reformer, but reviled for his ruthless tactics. Having learned modern ways as the ambassador to Britain, he battled Church repression and promoted the democratic ideals of the Enlightenment, but enforced his policies with arrests, torture, and executions. He expelled the Jesuits to keep them from monopolizing the education system, put the bishop of Coimbra in prison, and broke off relations with the pope. When the earthquake of 1755 leveled the city, within a month Pombal had kicked off major rebuilding in much of today's historic downtown—featuring a grid plan for the world's first quake-proof buildings. In 1777, the king died and the controversial Pombal was dismissed.

chance to enjoy the Manueline architecture. When you finally leave the castle complex grounds (at the little statue of St. George), jog to the left 30 yards past the gate, turn right on Travessa de São Bartolomeu, which becomes Travessa do Chão da Feira, and follow the striped lane downhill through Largo do Contador Mor (a small, car-clogged square with a Parisian ambience that has two handy outdoor restaurants, with grilled sardines as their specialty. Continue downhill 50 yards farther, pass the trolley tracks, circle right around the little church, to reach a superb Alfama viewpoint at...

❺ Largo Santa Luzia

From this square (a stop for trolleys #12E and #28E), admire the panoramic view from the small terrace, Miradouro de Santa Luzia, where old-timers play cards amid lots of tiles.

In the distance to the left, the **Vasco da Gama Bridge** (opened in 1998) connects Lisbon with new, modern bedroom communities south of the river. Below, the purple building with the green shades marks the square called Largo de São Miguel—the center of the Alfama. Where the Alfama neighborhood hits the river, notice the recently built embankment. It reclaimed 100 yards of land from the river to make a modern port, used these days to accommodate Lisbon's growing cruise ship industry.

On the wall of the church (facing the little view park) find two 18th-century tiles. One (on the left) shows Praça do Comércio before the 1755 earthquake. The 16th-century royal palace (shown on the left of the tilework, where the king went after abandoning the castle) was completely destroyed in the quake. The other tile (on the right) depicts the reconquest of Lisbon from the Moors by Afonso Henriques, described earlier. You can see the Portuguese hero, Martim Moniz, who let himself be crushed in the castle door to hold it open for his comrades. Notice the panicky Moors inside realizing that their castle is about to be breeched by invading Crusaders. It was a bad day for the Moors.

For an even better city view, hike back around the church and walk out to the seaside end of the Miradouro de Largo das Portas do Sol catwalk. The huge building dominating the neighborhood on the far left is the Monastery of São Vicente, constructed around 1600 by the Spanish king, Philip II, who wanted to leave his mark with this tribute to St. Vincent. A few steps away, under a statue of St. Vincent, is a kiosk café where you can enjoy perhaps the most scenic cup of coffee in town (daily 10:00-18:00).

• *Across the street from the café, you'll find the...*

➏ Museum and School of Portuguese Decorative Arts

The Museum and School of Portuguese Decorative Arts (Museu Escola de Artes Decorativas Portuguesas) offers a unique stroll through an aristocratic household, richly decorated in 16th- to 19th-century styles. In 1947, Ricardo do Espirito Santo Silva restored this Azurura Palace to house his collection of 15th- to 18th-century fine art, and then willed it to the state. He created perhaps the best chance for visitors to experience what an aristocratic home looked like during Lisbon's glory days. The coach at the ground level is "Berlin style," with a state-of-the-art suspension system. The grand stairway leads past 18th-century glazed tiles (Chinese-style blue-and-white was in vogue) upstairs into a world rich in colonial riches. Portuguese aristocrats had a flair for "Indo-Portuguese" decorative arts: exotic woods, shells, and Oriental porcelain (€4, Wed-Mon 10:00-17:00, closed Tue, Largo das Portas do Sol 2, tel. 218-814-640, www.fress.pt).

• *From here, it's downhill all the way. From Largo das Portas do Sol (the plaza with the statue of local patron St. Vincent, near the kiosk café on the terrace), go down the stairs (Rua Norberto de Araújo, between the church and the catwalk). The massive eighth-century fortified wall (on the right) once marked the boundary of Moorish Lisbon. Consider that the great stones on your right were stacked here over a thousand years ago. At the bottom of the wall, continue downhill, then turn left at the railing...and go down more stairs. Explore downhill from here.*

The main thoroughfare, a concrete stepped lane called Escadinhas de São Miguel, leads to the Alfama's main square, and...

❼ The Heart of the Alfama

This square, Largo de São Miguel, is the best place to observe a slice of Alfama life. While city leaders rebuilt the rest of Lisbon after the 1755 quake, this neighborhood was left out and consequently retains its tangled medieval street plan.

If you've got the time, explore the Alfama from this central square. Its urban-jungle roads are squeezed into confusing alleys—the labyrinthine street plan was designed to frustrate invaders and guidebook researchers trying to get up to the castle. What was defensive then is atmospheric now. Bent houses comfort each other in their romantic shabbiness, and the air drips with laundry and the smell of clams. Get lost. Poke aimlessly, peek through windows, buy a fish. Locals hang plastic water bags from windows in the summer to try to keep away the flies. Favorite saints decorate doors to protect families. St. Peter, protector of fishermen, is big in the Alfama. Churches are generally closed, since they share a priest. As children have very little usable land for a good soccer game, goalposts are painted onto the stairs. The tiny balconies were limited to "one-and-a-half hands" in width. A strictly enforced health initiative kept the town open and well-ventilated. If you see carpets hanging out to dry, it means a laundry is nearby. Because few homes have their own, every neighborhood has a public laundry and bathroom. Until recently, in the early morning hours, the streets were busy with residents in pajamas, heading for these public baths. Today, many are choosing to live elsewhere, lured by modern conveniences unavailable here, and the old flats became congested with immigrant laborers (mostly Ukrainian and Brazilian) who came during the construction boom a decade ago. Today, with the bad economy, they are moving on in search of employment. In just a couple of generations, the demographics have changed—from fishermen's families to immigrants to young bohemians.

Traditionally the neighborhood here was tightly knit, with families routinely sitting down to communal dinners in the streets. Feuds, friendships, and gossip were all intense. Historically, when a woman's husband died, she wore black for the rest of her life—a tradition that's just about gone.

The Alfama hosts Lisbon's most popular outdoor party on St. Anthony's Day (June 13). Imagine tables set up everywhere, bands playing, bright plastic flowers strung across the squares, and all the grilled sardines *(sardinhas grelhadas)* you can eat. The rustic paintings of festive characters (with hints of Moorish style) remind locals of past parties, and strings and wires overhead await future festival dates when the neighborhood will again be festooned with colorful streamers.

While there are plenty of traditional festivals here, the most action on the Alfama calendar is the insane, annual mountain-bike street race from the castle to the sea (which you can see hurtle by in under two minutes on YouTube; search "Lisboa downtown race").

• *Continue exploring downhill from here. You'll see a trendy little restaurant (the recommended Restaurante Santo Antonio de Alfama) and the recommended amateur fado restaurant (A Baiuca). Then, a few steps below the square, you'll hit the cobbled pedestrian lane, Rua São Pedro. This darkest of the Alfama's streets, in nearly perpetual shade, was the logical choice for the neighborhood's fish market. Modern hygiene requirements (which forbid outdoor stalls) killed the market, but it's still a characteristic lane to explore. Turn left and follow Rua São Pedro out of the Alfama to the square called Largo do Chafariz de Dentro and, across the street, the...*

❽ Fado Museum

This museum, rated ▲, tells the story of fado in English—with a great chance to hear these wailing fisherwomen's blues. Three levels of wall murals show three generations of local fado stars, and the audioguide lets you hear the Billie Holidays of Portugal (€5, includes audioguide, Tue-Sun 10:00-18:00, closed Mon, last entry 30 minutes before closing, Largo do Chafariz de Dentro, tel. 218-823-470, www.museudofado.pt).

• *This walk is over. To get back downtown (or to Praça do Comércio, where the next walk starts) from the Fado Museum, walk a block to the main waterfront drag and cruise-ship harbor (facing museum, go left around it) where busy Avenida Infante Dom Henrique leads back to Praça do Comércio downtown. While it's a 15-minute walk or quick taxi ride to Praça do Comércio, just to the left is a bus stop. Ride any bus for two stops and you're there in moments. (Also, bus #759 goes on to Praça dos Restauradores; #9, #90, and #746 continue up Avenida da Liberdade.)*

▲▲▲THE BAIXA STROLL: LISBON'S HISTORIC DOWNTOWN

This walk covers the highlights of Lisbon's downtown, the Baixa, which fills the flat valley between two hills, sloping gently from the waterfront up to the Rossio, Praça dos Restauradores, Avenida da Liberdade, and the newer town. The walk starts at Praça do Comércio and ends at Praça dos Restauradores.

After the disastrous 1755 earthquake, the Baixa district was

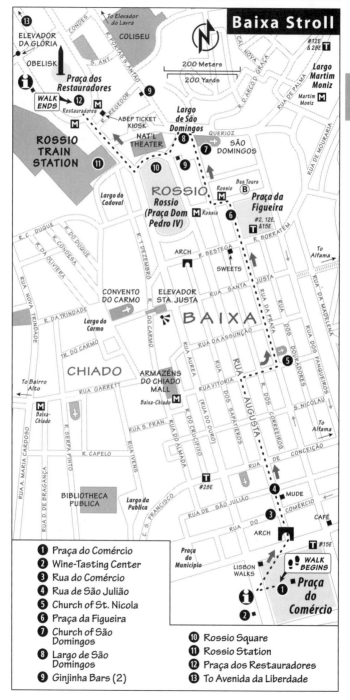

Baixa Stroll

LISBON

- ❶ Praça do Comércio
- ❷ Wine-Tasting Center
- ❸ Rua do Comércio
- ❹ Rua de São Julião
- ❺ Church of St. Nicola
- ❻ Praça da Figueira
- ❼ Church of São Domingos
- ❽ Largo de São Domingos
- ❾ Ginjinha Bars (2)
- ❿ Rossio Square
- ⓫ Rossio Station
- ⓬ Praça dos Restauradores
- ⓭ To Avenida da Liberdade

rebuilt on a grid street plan. The uniform and utilitarian Pombaline architecture (named after the Marquês
de Pombal, the prime minister who
rebuilt the city—see sidebar, earlier)
feels almost military. That's because
it is. The Baixa was built by military
engineers who had experience build-
ing garrison towns overseas. The new Lisbon featured the architecture of conquest—simple to assemble, economical, with all the
pieces easy to ship. The 18th-century buildings you'd see in Mozambique and Brazil are interchangeable with those in Lisbon.

The buildings are all uniform, with the same number of floors
and standard facades. They were designed to survive the next
earthquake, with stone firewalls and wooden frameworks featuring crisscross beams that flexed. The priorities were to rebuild fast,
cheap, and earthquake-proof.

If it were left up to the people, who believed the earthquake
was a punishment from God, they would have rebuilt their churches bigger and more impressive than ever. But Pombal was a practical military man with a budget, a timeline, and an awareness of his
society's limits. He didn't want church-building to compromise the
needs of the people. In those austere post-earthquake days, Pombal
got his way.

The Baixa has three squares: two pre-earthquake (Comércio
and Rossio) and one added later (Figueira), and three main streets:
Prata (silver), Aurea (gold), and Augusta (relating the Portuguese
king to a Roman emperor). The former maze of the Jewish Quarter
was eliminated, but the area has many streets named for the crafts
and shops once found there.

The Baixa's pedestrian streets, inviting cafés, bustling shops,
and elegant old storefronts give the district a certain charm. City-
government subsidies make sure the old businesses stay around,
but modern ones find a way to creep in. I find myself doing laps up
and down Rua Augusta in a people-watching stupor. Its delightful
ambience is perfect for strolling and reminiscent of the Ramblas in
Barcelona.

• *Start your walk under the statue of King José I in the center of Praça
do Comércio.*

❶ Praça do Comércio
("Trade Square")

At this riverfront square bordering the Baixa—long the gateway
to Lisbon—ships used to dock and sell their goods. Nicknamed
"Palace Square" by locals, it was the site of Portugal's royal palace
for 200 pre-earthquake years. After the 1755 earthquake/tsunami/

fire, the jittery king fled to more-stable Belém, never to return. These days, government ministries ring Praça do Comércio. It's also the departure point for city bus and tram tours, and boats that cruise along the Rio Tejo. The area opposite the harbor was conceived as a residential neighborhood for the upper class, but they chose the suburbs. Today, the square has two names ("Palace Square" and "Commercial Square") and little real life. Locals consider it just a big place to pass through.

The statue is of King José I, the man who gave control of the government to Pombal, who rebuilt the city after the earthquake. Built 20 years after the quake, it shows the king on his horse, with Pombal (on the medallion), looking at their port. The horse (symbolic of triumph) stomps on snakes (symbolic of evil—perhaps Protestants...or troublemaking noble families), while the elephant represents the Portuguese empire's colonies in India and Africa. In its glory days, this city was where east met west.

The big arch marking the inland side of the square is Lisbon's Arch of Triumph (with Vasco da Gama on the left and Pombal on the right). Disregarding his usual austerity, Pombal restored some of the city's Parisian-style grandeur at this central approach into downtown.

Note there are two tourist sights on the square, neither worth your time nor money. The much-promoted "Lisbon Story Center" is a childish exhibit with no artifacts—you pay €7 to stand for an hour looking at animated history on computer screens. The towering Rua Augusta Arch is open to climb (€2.50, elevator plus 74 steps), but affords only a mediocre view from its empty rooftop.

• *With your back to the harbor (facing the Arch of Triumph), the TI, Vini Portugal wine-tasting center, and meeting point for walking tours are on your left; and the Terriero do Paço Metro stop is behind you on the right (in the southeast corner of the square).*

❷ Wine-Tasting Center

At the **Wines of Portugal Tasting Room**, the country's vintners sponsor a nonprofit wine-appreciation venue. Sixteen local wines are offered with English descriptions above each tap, with a helpful attendant happy to explain things. To taste, you buy a chip card (€2 minimum), are given a glass, and serve yourself various samples of eight whites and eight reds from €0.50 and up (Tue-Sat 11:00-19:00, closed Sun-Mon, next to TI).

Martinho da Arcada, a fine option for a coffee, pastry, or snack, is under the arcades on Praça do Comércio. It was founded in 1782—when the wealthy would come here to savor early ice cream made with mountain snow, lemon, and spices. While it has a fancy restaurant, I'd enjoy just coffee and pastry in its café bar. This place was one of poet Fernando Pessoa's old haunts (they display a few Pessoa artifacts). In the early 20th century, painters, writers, and dreamers shared revolutionary ideas here over coffee (Praça do Comércio 8, at the corner of Rua da Prata).

• *Pass through the big arch and walk down Rua Augusta into the Baixa district. The next two stops along this walk take you straight down Rua Augusta, pausing at three cross streets.*

❸ Rua do Comércio

Look right to see the old cathedral with its Romanesque fortress-like crenellations. Notice that many of the surrounding buildings are austere, with no tiles—this was the architectural style adopted immediately after the earthquake, when only the interiors of buildings were tiled. In the Portuguese colony of Brazil, people found that tiles protected against humidity, and eventually (by the 19th century), tilework was adopted as a form of exterior decoration here in Lisbon.

The characteristic black-and-white cobbled sidewalk *(calçada)* is uniquely Portuguese. These mosaic limestone and basalt cobbles were first cut and laid by 19th-century prison laborers. To this day patterns are chosen from a book of acceptable designs. As the stones are slippery and expensive to maintain, the city government is talking about replacing them with modern pavement. And locals are crying out to keep the tradition.

Across the street, on the right, you'll pass the Museum la Mode, Lisbon's museum of design (a.k.a. MUDE; free, Tue-Sun 10:00-18:00, closed Mon). Filling the Art Deco ground floor of a former bank, it offers a quick, one-floor stroll through 20th-century fashion. Special exhibits are on other floors, and a huge bank vault in the basement is often part of the show.

• *At Rua de São Julião, look left about 30 yards and try to find the church—it's hiding.*

❹ Rua de São Julião

Churches are scarce in the post-earthquake Baixa. Only a few of the churches destroyed by the quake were permitted to be rebuilt. The replacement churches were incorporated into the no-nonsense military style, with facades that match the rest of the street. You'll notice that the Baixa district is struggling to stay vital, with the upper floors of many buildings now mostly empty. Look up for evidence of how downtown Lisbon's population is shrinking, as more people move to the suburbs.

LISBON

The Lisbon Earthquake of 1755

At 9:40 in the morning on Sunday, November 1—All Saints' Day—an earthquake estimated to be close to 9.0 in magnitude rumbled through the city, punctuated by three main jolts. Its arrival came midway through Mass. Ten minutes later, thousands lay dead under the rubble.

Along the waterfront, shaken survivors scrambled aboard boats to sail to safety. They were met by a 20-foot wall of water, the first wave of a tsunami that rushed up the Rio Tejo. The ravaging water capsized ships, swept people off the docks, crested over the seawall, and crashed 800 feet inland.

After the quake, the city turned into an inferno, as overturned cooking fires and fallen candles ignited raging fires. The fires blazed for five days, ravaging the downtown from the Bairro Alto across Rossio to the castle atop the Alfama.

Of Lisbon's 270,000 citizens, over 10,000 may have perished. Besides leveling the city, the quake shook conservative Portugal's moral and spiritual underpinnings. Had God punished Lisbon for the Inquisition killings carried out on nearby Praça do Comércio?

King José I was so affected by the earthquake that he moved his entire court to an elaborate complex of tents in the foothills of Belém and resisted living indoors for the rest of his life.

At the next block, the handy trolley #28E stops at Rua da Conceição. Ahead on the right (in the windows of the Millennium Bank) are Roman artifacts—a reminder that Lisbon's history goes way back.

• *At Rua da Vitoria, turn right and walk to Rua da Prata, where you'll see the camouflaged...*

❺ Church of St. Nicola (Igreja de São Nicolau)

Notice how its church-like facade was allowed, but the entire green-tiled side is disguised as just another stretch of post-earthquake Baixa architecture.

• *Head left down Rua da Prata toward the statue marking Praça da Figueira. At Rua de Santa Justa, look left for a good view of Elevador de Santa Justa before continuing straight to the square.*

❻ Praça da Figueira ("Fig Tree Square")

This was the site of a huge hospital destroyed in the earthquake. With no money to replace the hospital, the space was left open until the late 1880s, when it was filled with a big iron-framed market (similar to Barcelona's La Boqueria). That structure was torn down decades ago, leaving the square you see today. The big building on the left is run-down—after 50 years of rent control, many landowners are demoralized and do nothing to fix up their property. Buildings like this are often either vacant or occupied by old pensioners living out their lives amid increasingly decrepit conditions. By contrast, the right side (under the castle) is more lived-in and vibrant.

The nearby **Confeitaria Nacional** shop (on the corner of the square, 20 yards to your left) is a venerable palace of sweets little changed since the 19th century. In the window is a display of *"conventuel* sweets"—special nun-made treats often consisting of sugar and egg yolks (historically, the nuns, who used the egg whites to starch their laundry, had an abundance of yolks). Consider a light lunch here in the upstairs dining room.

The square is a transportation hub, with stops for the minibus #737 and the old trolley #12E going to the castle, the modern trolley #15E and bus #714 heading out to Belém, and the touristic hop-on, hop-off buses.

• *Walk to the far-left corner of the square, past skateboarders oblivious to its historical statue—Portugal's King John I on a horse. Leave the square down the Rua Dom Antão de Almada. This lane has several characteristic shops. Pop into the classic cod shop (on the left at #1C—you'll smell it). Cod is part of Portugal's heritage as a nation of seafaring explorers: It was salted and could keep for a year on a ship. Just soak in water to rinse out the salt and enjoy. The adjacent ham counter serves pata negra (presunto ibérico) from acorn-fed pigs—the very best. The non-pork alheira sausage is made with game and was a favorite among Lisbon's Jews back when they needed to fake being Christians. At the end of the lane stands a big church facing another square.*

❼ Church of São Domingos

A center of the Inquisition in the 1600s, this is now one of Lisbon's most active churches (daily 7:30-19:00). The evocative interior—more or less rebuilt from the ruins left by the 1755 earthquake—reminds visitors of that horrible All Saints' Day Sunday, when most of the city was at Mass and the earth rolled. Across the city, heavy stone church walls like these collapsed on their congregations. Standing at the back of the nave, you can see which parts of the pre-1755 stone walls remained standing afterward. The black soot on the walls and the charred stonework at the altar recalls the horrible fires that followed the earthquake. Our Lady of Fátima is Portugal's most popular saint. Her chapel (in the left rear of the church) always has the most candles. She's accompanied by two of the three children

who saw the miraculous apparition (the third was still alive when this chapel was made and so is not shown in heaven with the saint).
• *Step into the square just beyond the church.*

❽ Largo de São Domingos

This area was just outside of the old town walls—long a place where people gathered to keep watering holes busy and enjoy bohemian entertainment. Today the square is home to classic old bars (a *ginjinha* bar is described next) and a busy "eating lane," Rua das Portas de Santo Antão (kitty-corner from where you entered the square, to the right of the National Theater on the far side of the square).

The square once held a palace that functioned as the head-quarters of the Inquisition. It was demolished, and in an attempt to erase its memory, the National Theater was built in its place. The city massacred the town's Jews on this square in 1506. A stone monument, unveiled in 2008, remembers this sad event.

Once the site of Lisbon's 16th-century slave market, this square is now a meeting point for the city's African immigrant community—people from former Portuguese colonies such as Angola, Mozambique, and Portuguese Guinea. They hang out, trade news from home, and watch the tourists go by.
• *Find the colorful little hole-in-the-wall tavern facing the square and serving the traditional cherry brandy.*

❾ Liquid Sightseeing

Ginjinha (zheen-ZHEEN-yah) is a favorite Lisbon drink. While nuns baked sweets, the monks took care of quenching thirsts with this sweet liquor, made from the sour cherry-like *ginja* berry, sugar, cinnamon, and brandy. It's now sold for €1.10 a shot in funky old shops throughout downtown. Buy it with or without berries (*com elas* or *sem elas*—that's "with them" or "without them") and *gelada* (if you want it poured from a chilled bottle). In Portugal, when people are impressed by the taste of something, they say, *"Sabe que nem ginjas"*—literally "It tastes like *ginja*," but meaning "finger-lickin' good." The oldest *ginjinha* joint in town is a colorful hole-in-the-wall at Largo de São Domingos 8. If you hang around the bar long enough, you'll see them refill the bottle from an enormous vat. (Another *ginjinha* bar, named for Eduardino the clown and considered the most authentic, is a block away on the restaurant row, Rua das Portas de Santo Antão, next to #59; daily 7:00-24:00.)
• *The big square around the corner (fronting the National Theater) is Rossio.*

⑩ Rossio

Lisbon's historic center, Rossio, is still the city's bustling cultural heart. Given its elongated shape, historians believe it was a Roman racetrack 2,000 years ago; these days, cars circle the loop instead of chariots. It's home to the colonnaded National Theater, a McDonald's, and street vendors who can shine your shoes, laminate your documents, and sell you cheap watches, autumn chestnuts, and lottery tickets. The column in the square's center honors Pedro IV—king of Portugal and emperor of Brazil. (Many maps refer to the square as Praça Dom Pedro IV, but residents always just call it Rossio, referring to the train station at one corner.)

From here you can see the Elevador de Santa Justa and the ruined convent breaking the city skyline. Notice the fine stone patterns in the pavement—evoking waves encountered by the great explorers—which once upon a time made locals seasick.

• *Crossing the square in front of the National Theater, you see Rossio Station.*

⑪ Rossio Station

The circa-1900 facade of Rossio Station is Neo-Manueline. You can read the words *Central Station* printed on its striking horseshoe arches. Find the statue of King Sebastian in the center of two arches. This romantic, dashing, and young soldier king was lost in 1580 in an ill-fated crusade in Africa. As Sebastian left no direct

heir, the crown ended up with Philip II of Spain, who became Philip I of Portugal. The Spanish king promised to give back the throne if Sebastian ever turned up—and ever since, the Portuguese have dreamed that Sebastian will return, restoring their national greatness. Even today, in a crisis, the Portuguese like to think that their Sebastian will save the day—he's the symbol of being ridiculously hopeful.

• *Just uphill from Rossio Station is Praça dos Restauradores, at the bottom of Lisbon's long and grand Avenida da Liberdade.*

⑫ Praça dos Restauradores

This monumental square connects Rossio with Avenida da Liberdade (described next). Its centerpiece, an obelisk, celebrates the restoration of Portuguese independence from Spain in 1640 (without any help from the still-missing Sebastian mentioned earlier).

Just off the square is Lisbon's oldest hotel (the Hotel Avenida Palace, built as a terminus hotel at the same time as Rossio Station), the 1920s Art Deco facade of the Eden Theater, a TI, a green ABEP kiosk (selling tickets for concerts, movies, bullfights, and sports events) at the southern end, the Elevador da Glória funicular that climbs to the Bairro Alto (a bit up the street, opposite the Hard Rock Café), and a Metro station. A block to the east is Lisbon's "eating lane" (Rua das Portas de Santo Antão), the restaurant-lined street mentioned earlier.

• *While this walk ends here, stroll up Avenida da Liberdade for a good look at another facet of this fine city.*

⓭ Avenida da Liberdade

This tree-lined grand boulevard, running north from Rossio, connects the old town (where most of the sightseeing action is) with the newer upper town. Before the great earthquake, this was the city's royal promenade. After 1755, it was the grand boulevard of Pombal's new Lisbon—originally limited to the aristocracy. The present street, built in the 1880s and inspired by Paris' Champs-Elysées, is lined with banks, airline offices, nondescript office buildings...and eight noisy lanes of traffic. The grand "rotunda"—as the roundabout formally known as Marquês de Pombal is called—tops off the Avenida da Liberdade with a commanding statue of Pombal. Allegorical symbols of his impressive accomplishments decorate the statue. (A single-minded dictator can do a lot in 27 years.) Beyond that lies the fine Edward VII Park. From the Rotunda (Metro: Marquês de Pombal), it's an enjoyable 20-minute downhill walk along the mile-long avenue back to the Baixa.

▲▲▲THE BAIRRO ALTO AND CHIADO STROLL

Rise above the Baixa on the funicular, Elevador da Glória, located near the obelisk at Praça dos Restauradores (opposite the Hard Rock Café, €3.60 if you pay driver, cheaper with Viva Viagem card, 6/hour); you can also hike up alongside the tracks.

• *Leaving the funicular on top, turn right (go 100 yards, up into a park) to enjoy the city view from the...*

❶ Miradouro de São Pedro de Alcântara (San Pedro Belvedere)

The tile map guides you through the view, stretching from the twin towers of the cathedral (Sé, on far right behind trees), to the ramparts of the castle birthplace of Lisbon (capping the hill, on right), to another quaint, tree-topped viewpoint in Graça (directly across, end of trolley #28E), to the skyscraper towers of the new city in the distance (on far left). Note that whenever you see a big old building in Lisbon, it's often a former convent or monastery, nationalized by the state, and now occupied by a hospital, school, or the military.

In the park, a bust honors a 19th-century local journalist (founder of Lisbon's first daily newspaper) and a charming, bare-footed delivery boy. This district is famous for its writers, poets, publishers, and bohemians. (The walk continues downhill from here.)

• Directly across the street from where you got off the Elevador da Glória is the...

❼ Port Wine Institute

If you're into port (the fortified wine that takes its name from the city of Porto, covered later in this book), you'll find the world's greatest selection at **Solar do Vinho do Porto,** run by the Port Wine Institute (Mon-Sat 11:00-24:00, closed Sun, WCs, Rua São Pedro de Alcântara 45, tel. 213-475-707). You're welcome to go in to simply browse even if you're not drinking. The plush, air-conditioned, Old World living room is furnished with leather chairs (this is not a shorts-and-T-shirt kind of place). You can order from a selection of more than 150 different ports (€1.50-22 per glass), generally poured by an English-speaking bartender. Read the instructive menu for an education in port. Fans of port describe it as "a liquid symphony playing on the palate." Browse through the easy menu. Start white and sweet (cheapest), taste your way through spicy and ruby, and finish mellow and tawny. A *colheita* (single harvest) is particularly good. Appetizers *(aperitivos)* are listed in the menu with small photographs. Seated service can be slow and disinterested when it's busy. As these are government employees and their jobs are secure, smiles are unnecessary. To be served without a long wait, go to the bar. Enjoy the Douro Valley photos, maps, and models of traditional boats that add to the port-industry ambience of the place.

• Next, side-trip directly across from the top of the funicular into the old grid-plan streets of the Bairro Alto. While it's fun to wander, follow this route for a good sampling: Go three blocks uphill, turn left on Rua da Atalaia, continue three blocks, and then head left down Travessa da Queimada until you cross the big street (leaving the Bairro Alto) and reach the small square, Largo Trindade Coelho.

❽ Bairro Alto Detour

The "High Town," or Bairro Alto, is one of the most characteristic and charming districts in Lisbon. While the Baixa (lower town) has a grid plan because it was rebuilt after the 1755 earthquake, the Bairro Alto was designed in the 16th century with a very modern (at the time) grid-plan layout. The district housed ship work-

LISBON

Bairro Alto Stroll

WALK BEGINS

ELEVADOR DA GLÓRIA

São Pedro de Alcântara Park

OBELISK

Praça dos Restauradores

Restauradores

ABEP TICKET KIOSK

To Elevador do Lavra

COLISEU

NAT'L THEATER

Largo de São Domingos

ROSSIO

ROSSIO TRAIN STATION

Rossio (Praça Dom Pedro IV)

IGREJA SÃO ROQUE

MUSEU DE ARTE SACRA

Largo do Cadoval

BAIXA

Largo Trindade Coelho

CONVENTO DO CARMO

ELEVADOR STA. JUSTA

ARCH

BAIRRO ALTO

TEATRO DA TRINDADE

Largo do Carmo

To Miradouro de Santa Caterina

ELEVADOR DA BICA

Praça Camões #28E

WALK ENDS

CHIADO

ARMAZÉNS DO CHIADO MALL

Baixa-Chiado

RUA GARRETT

BICA

BIBLIOTECA PUBLICA

Largo da Publica

To Baixa & Alfama

To Cais do Sodré Station

200 Meters

200 Yards

Praça do Município

#28E

1 Miradouro de São Pedro de Alcântara
2 Port Wine Institute
3 Bairro Alto Detour
4 São Roque Church
5 Cervejaria da Trindade
6 Largo do Carmo
7 Convento do Carmo
8 Elevador de Santa Justa
9 Café A Brasileira
10 A Vida Portuguesa Gift Shop
11 Armazéns do Chiado Mall

Lisbon's Kiosks

The kiosk—that's *quiosque* in Portuguese—has become a standard feature of squares and viewpoints all over town. Many originated a century ago as the city's first phone terminals. Later they became newsstands, lottery sales points, and now outdoor cafés turning parks and squares into neighborhood hangouts and meeting points. New ones are being built all the time and can be quite trendy. If you see a group of people talking, you'll likely notice a newsstand kiosk nearby—kiosks sell three daily newspapers devoted to football (soccer). With tough economic times, and what many consider a corrupt elite colluding with the government to keep the populace down, working-class people are conveniently distracted by sports.

ers back when Portugal was a world power and its ships planted the Portuguese flag all around the globe. Today, the Bairro Alto is quiet in the morning, but buzzes with a thriving restaurant scene in the evening.

• *On the square, Largo Trindade Coelho, is the...*

❹ São Roque Church

Step inside, and then sit on a pew in the middle to take it all in (free, Mon 14:00-18:00, Tue-Sun 9:00-18:00). Built in the 16th century, the church of St. Roque, worth ▲, is one of Portugal's first Jesuit churches. The painted wood, false-domed ceiling is perfectly flat. The acoustics here are top-notch, important in a Jesuit church, where the emphasis is on the sermon (given from twin pulpits mid-nave). The numbered panels on the floor were tombs, nameless because they were for lots of people. They're empty now—the practice was stopped in the 19th century when parishioners didn't want plague victims rotting under their feet.

Survey the rich side chapels. The highlight is the Chapel of St. John the Baptist (left of altar, gold and blue lapis lazuli columns). It looks like it came right out of the Vatican—and that's because it did. Made in Rome out of the most precious materials, the chapel was the site of one papal Mass; then it was disassembled and shipped to Lisbon. Per square inch, it was the most costly chapel ever constructed in Portugal. Notice the mosaic floor (with the spherical symbol of Portugal) and the three "paintings" that are actually intricate, beautiful mosaics—a Vatican specialty, designed to avoid damage from candle smoke that would darken real paintings. Notice also the delicate "sliced marble" symmetry and imagine the labor involved in so artfully cutting that stone five centuries ago. To the right, a glass case is filled with relics trying to grab your attention. The next chapel to the left features a riot of babies. Individual chapels—each for a different noble family—seem to be in competition. Keep in mind that the tiles are considered as extravagant as the gold leaf and silver.

To the right of the altar is the sacristy where, along with huge chests of drawers for vestments, you can see a series of 17th-century paintings illustrating scenes from the life of St. Frances Xavier—co-founder of the Jesuit order with St.Ignatius of Loyola.

The São Roque Museum (outside the church, to the left as you leave) is more interesting than your typical small church museum. It's filled with perhaps the best-presented collection of 16th- and 17th-century church art in town, and is well described in English. The church and this art, rare survivors of the 1755 earthquake, illustrate the religious passion that accompanied Portugal's Age of Discovery, with themes including: the mission of the Jesuits and their response to the Reformation; devotion to relics; and devotion to the Virgin (€2.50, same hours as the church).

• *Back outside in the church square (charming WC underground), visit the statue of a friendly lottery-ticket salesman. Two lottery kiosks are nearby. Locals who buy into the* totoloto *(which, like national lotteries everywhere, is a form of taxation on gamblers that helps fund government social programs) rub the statue's ticket for good luck. Continue (kitty-corner across the square) downhill along Rua Nova da Trindade. At #20, pop into...*

❺ Cervejaria da Trindade

The famous "oldest beer hall in Lisbon" is worth a visit for a look at its 19th-century tiles. The beautifully tiled main room, once a refectory (monks' dining hall), still holds the pulpit from which the Bible was read as the monks ate. After the monastery was abolished in 1836 it became a brewery—you'll notice that while the oldest tiles have Christian themes, the later ones (from around 1860) are all about the beer. They have five Portuguese beers on tap—Sagres is the standard lager, Sagres Preta is a good dark beer (like a porter), and Bohemia is sweet, with more alcohol. At the bar in front you can get a snack and beer, while more expensive dining is in the back.

When you're done, continue downhill to Livraria Barateira at #16, Lisbon's biggest used bookstore, where you can sell this book.

• *Continue down the hill, where at the next intersection, signs point left to the ruined Convento do Carmo. Follow the inside trolley tracks downhill and to the left to the next square...*

❻ Largo do Carmo

On this square decorated with an old fountain, lots of pigeons, and jacaranda trees from South America (with purple blossoms in June), police officers guard the headquarters of the National Guard.

Famous among residents, this was the last refuge of the fascist dictator António Salazar's successor. The Portuguese people won their revolution in 1974, in a peaceful uprising called the Carnation Revolution. The name came when revolutionaries placed flowers in the guns of the soldiers, making it clear it was time for democracy here. For more history, see the sidebar.

• *On Largo do Carmo, check out the ruins of...*

❼ Convento do Carmo

After the convent was destroyed by the 1755 earthquake, the Marquês de Pombal directed that the delicate Gothic arches of its church be left standing—supporting nothing but open sky—as a permanent reminder of that disastrous event. If you pay to enter, you'll see a fine memorial park in what was the nave, and a simple museum with Bronze Age and Roman artifacts, medieval royal sarcophagi, and a couple of Peruvian mummies—all explained in English (€3.50—cheapskates can do a deep knee-bend at the ticket desk, sneak a peek, and then crawl away; June-Sept Mon-Sat 10:00-19:00, Oct-May until 18:00, closed Sun year-round).

• *Just past the convent (to the right as you face it), a lane leads out and around to a fine city viewpoint from the top of the Elevador de Santa Justa.*

❽ Elevador de Santa Justa

In 1902, an architect—who studied under Gustav Eiffel—completed this 150-foot-tall iron elevator, connecting the lower and upper parts of town. The elevator's Neo-Gothic motifs are an attempt to match the ruined church near its top. While you'll need to pay extra to go to the top-floor lookout for a fine city view, the view from the entry-ramp level is nearly as good—and free (€5 round-trip ticket, free with Via Viagem card loaded with 24-hour pass—if "Zapping," it'll cost your card €1.40, daily 7:00-21:30).

Stroll around this celebration of the Industrial Age, enjoy the view, and retrace your steps to the square in front of the convent. (The nearby Leitaria Académica, a venerable little working-class eatery with tables spilling onto the delightful square, can be handy for a snack or drink.)

• *Leave Largo do Carmo, walking a block slightly uphill on Travessa do Carmo. At the next square, take a left on Rua Serpa Pinto, walking downhill to Rua Garrett, where—in the little pedestrian zone 50 yards uphill on the right—you'll find a famous old café across from the Baixa-Chiado Metro stop.*

❾ Café A Brasileira

Reeking of smoke and slinky with Art Nouveau decor, this café is a 100-year-old institution for coffeehouse junkies. Drop in for

The Carnation Revolution

António Salazar, who ruled Portugal from 1926 to 1968, was modern Europe's longest-ruling dictator (he died in 1970).

Salazar's authoritarian regime, the Estado Novo, continued in power under Prime Minister Marcelo Caetano until 1974.

By the 1970s, all the fighting in Portugal's far-flung colonies over the past decade had demoralized much of Salazar's military, and at home, there was a growing appetite for a modern democracy. On April 25, 1974, several prominent members of the military reluctantly sided with a growing popular movement to oust the government. Their withdrawal of support spelled the end of the Salazar era. Five people died that April day, in a well-planned, relatively bloodless coup. Citizens spilled into the streets to cheer and put flowers in soldiers' rifle barrels, giving the event its name: the Carnation Revolution. Suddenly, people were free to speak aloud what they formerly could only whisper in private.

In the revolution's aftermath, the country struggled to get the hang of modern democracy. Its economy suffered as overseas colonies fell to nationalist uprisings, flooding the country with some 800,000 emigrants. For colonial overlords, life went from "shrimp day and night" to a sudden collapse of the empire; for their own safety, they fled back to Portugal. A good number of these "returnees" didn't fit into their newly democratic old country—feeling like people without a homeland, many ultimately left Portugal (joining Salazar's henchmen, who took refuge in Brazil). Even those who stayed were generally pro-dictator and angry about the revolution, contributing to a polarization of modern Portuguese society that exists to this day.

In 1976, the Portuguese adopted a constitution that separated church and state. These changes helped to break down the almost-medieval class system and establish parliamentary law. Mario Soares, a former enemy of the Salazar regime, became the new prime minister, ruling as a stabilizing presence through much of the next two decades. Today, Portugal is enthusiastically democratic.

a *bica* (Lisbon slang for an espresso, €0.70 at the bar) and a €1.30 *pastel de nata* custard tart—a Lisbon specialty. (WCs are down the stairs near the entrance.) This café was the literary and creative soul of Lisbon in the 1920s and 1930s, when the country's avant-garde poets, writers, and painters would hang out here. The statue outside is of the poet Fernando Pessoa (see sidebar), making him a perpetual regular at this café. A Brasileira was originally a shop

Portugal's Two Greatest Poets

The Portuguese are justifiably proud of their two most famous poets, whose names, works, and memorials you may encounter in your travels.

Portugal's most important poet, **Luís de Camões** (1524-1580), was a Renaissance-age equivalent of the ancient Greek poet, Homer. Camões' masterpiece, *The Lusiads (Os Lusíadas)*, tells the story of an explorer far from home. But instead of Odysseus, this epic poem describes the journey of Vasco da Gama, the man who found the route from Europe to India. Camões—who had sailed to Morocco to fight the Moors (where he lost an eye), to Goa (where he was imprisoned for debt), and to China (where he was shipwrecked)—was uniquely qualified to write about Portugal's pursuit of empire on the high seas. For more on Camões, see page 69.

Fernando Pessoa (1888-1935) used multiple personas in his poetry. He'd take on the voice of a simple countryman and

express his love of nature in free verse. Or he'd write as an erudite scholar, sharing philosophical thoughts in a more formal style. By varying his voice, he was able to more easily explore different viewpoints and truths. While Pessoa loved the classics—reading Milton, Byron, Shelley, and Poe—he was a true 20th-century bohemian at heart. Café A Brasileira, where he'd often meet with friends, has a statue of Pessoa outside. Today, fado musicians still remember Pessoa, paying homage to him by putting his poetry into the Portuguese version of the blues.

selling Brazilian products, a reminder that this has long been the city's shopping zone.

At the neighboring Baixa-Chiado (shee-AH-doo) Metro stop, a slick series of escalators whisks people effortlessly between Chiado Square and the Baixa (the lower town). It's a free and fun way to survey a long, long line of Portuguese—but for now, we'll stay in the Chiado neighborhood. (If you'll be coming for fado in the evening—recommended places are nearby—consider getting here by zipping up the escalator.)

The Chiado District is popular for its shopping and theaters. Browse downhill on Rua Garrett and notice its mosaic sidewalks, ironwork balconies, and fine shops. Peek into classy stores, such as the fabric-lover's paradise Paris em Lisboa—imagine how this would have been the ultimate in oo-la-la fashion in the 19th century (at #77). The venerable Bertrand bookstore (at #73) sells English books and has a good guidebook selection in Room 5. My favorite shop for traditional and retro Portuguese gifts is behind the bookstore: ❿ **A Vida Portuguesa** (daily 10:00-20:00, Rua Anchieta 11). The street lamps you see are decorated with the symbol of Lisbon: a ship, carrying the remains of St. Vincent, guarded by two ravens. In 1988, much of this area was destroyed in a fire.

• *Rua Garrett ends abruptly at the entrance of the big vertical mall. For Italian-style gelato, locals like* Santini em Casa, *a few steps downhill to the left (at #9, 30 yards below mall entry). Step into the fancy...*

⓫ **Armazéns do Chiado Mall:** This grand, six-floor shopping center connects Lisbon's lower and upper towns with a world of ways to spend money (daily 10:00-22:00, lively food court on sixth floor open daily about 12:00-23:00).

• *This walk is over. Whether you leave the Bairro Alto or stay to explore, directions are below.*

Leaving the Bairro Alto: *To get from the mall to the Baixa—the lower town—take the elevator (press 1) or the escalators down (to exit on the ground level, you'll pass through the Sports Zone shop). To get from the mall to the Metro, exit through the lowest floor of the mall, turn right, and walk 50 yards to the Baixa-Chiado Metro stop.*

Exploring More of the Bairro Alto: *A short walk from the mall gives you a more complete look at this high-altitude neighborhood and a scenic viewpoint. Get out your map and backtrack (heading west) up Rua Garrett (which becomes Rua do Loreto), passing the picturesque Elevador da Bica funicular, then turn left on Rua Marechal Saldanha to reach the Miradouro de Santa Catarina (a.k.a. the "Bica mirador"), a terrace—flanked by bars—that overlooks the city's harbor and river. You'll see a monument to the Cape of Good Hope (a.k.a. the Cape of Torment) that personifies the cape as a monster. This mythic treatment was popularized by poet Camões' The Lusiads, which celebrated and nearly deified the great explorers of Portugal's Age of Discovery (such as Vasco da Gama, portrayed as Ulysses), who had to overcome such demons in their conquest of the sea.*

LISBON

Sights in Lisbon

CENTRAL LISBON

To get a full picture of the best of central Lisbon, take the "Three Neighborhoods" walk (the Bairro Alto, Alfama, and Baixa) covered earlier.

Cathedral (Sé)

The cathedral, just a few blocks east of Praça do Comércio, is not much on the inside, but its fortress-like exterior—solid enough to survive the 1755 earthquake—is a textbook example of the stark and powerful Romanesque "fortress of God" so typical of its age. Twin, castle-like, crenellated towers solidly frame an impressive rose window.

Cost and Hours: Church—free, Tue-Sat 9:00-19:00, Sun-Mon 9:00-17:00; cloister—€2.50, Tue-Sat 10:00-18:30, Mon 10:00-17:00, closed Sun; treasury—€2.50, €4 combo-ticket includes cloister; on Largo da Sé, several blocks east of Baixa—take Rua da Conceição east, which turns into Rua de Santo António da Sé.

Visiting the Church: Started in 1150, this was the first place of worship that Christians built after they retook Lisbon from the Moors. Located on the former site of a mosque, it made a powerful statement: The Reconquista was here to stay. The church is also the site of the 1195 baptism of St. Anthony—a favorite saint of Portugal (locals appeal to him for help in finding a parking spot, true love, and lost objects). Naturally for Portugal, tile panels around the baptismal font portray St. Anthony preaching to the fish. Also, some of St. Vincent is buried here—legend has it that in the 12th century, his remains were brought to Lisbon on a ship guarded by two sacred black ravens, the symbol of the city.

The **cloister** at the right side of the church is peaceful and an archaeological work-in-progress—they're currently uncovering Roman ruins. The humble **treasury** is worth its fee only if you want to support the church and climb some stairs.

Elevador de Santa Justa

This 150-foot-tall iron tower, built in 1902, connects the flat Baixa district with the Bairro Alto/Chiado districts up above. You can ride the elevator for a fine city view, while getting a sweat-free connection to the upper town (€5 round-trip tickets only; covered by Viva Viagem card—a great value with 24-hour card which makes it free, if "Zapping," it'll cost your card €1.40; departures every 10 minutes, daily 7:00-23:00, until 22:00 in winter).

NORTH LISBON
▲▲▲Gulbenkian Museum

This is the best of Lisbon's 40 museums. It's two miles north of the city center, and worth the trip for art lovers. Calouste Gulbenkian (1869-1955), an Armenian oil tycoon, gave Portugal his art collection (or "harem," as he called it). His gift was an act of gratitude for the hospitable asylum granted him during World War II (he lived in Lisbon from 1942 until he died in 1955). The Portuguese consider Gulbenkian—whose billion-dollar estate is still a growing and vital arts foundation promoting culture in Portugal—an inspirational model of how to be thoughtfully wealthy. (He made a habit of "tithing for art," spending 10 percent of his income on things of beauty.) The foundation, with its building set in a delightful garden, often hosts classical music concerts in the museum's auditoriums.

Gulbenkian's collection, spanning 5,000 years and housed in a classy modern building, offers the most purely enjoyable museum experience in Iberia—it's both educational and just plain beautiful. The museum is cool, uncrowded, gorgeously lit, and easy to grasp, displaying only a few select and exquisite works from each epoch. Walk through five millennia of human history, appreciating our ancestors by seeing objects they treasured.

Cost and Hours: €5, free on Sun; open Tue-Sun 10:00-18:00, closed Mon, last entry 30 minutes before closing; terse 1.5-hour audioguide-€4, pleasant gardens, good air-conditioned cafeteria, Berna 45, tel. 217-823-000, www.museu.gulbenkian.pt.

Getting There: From downtown, hop a cab (€7) or take the Metro from Restauradores to the São Sebastião stop, get off, and leave the platform by following the *Avenida de Aguiar (norte)* signs. Then, to leave the station, follow signs to *Avenida de Aguiar (nascente)*. Once at street level, walk a long block downhill on Avenida de Aguiar with the massive El Corte Inglés department store behind you. Just before the roundabout (across from the funky, pink Spanish embassy on the left), you'll see a small sign pointing right to the *fundação*—the museum entrance is straight ahead through this park, past a long concrete office building, about 100 yards away.

Nearby: A fine modern art gallery (CAMJAP) is next door. And Belém is a quick €8 taxi ride away.

⊙ Self-Guided Tour: From the entrance lobby, there are two

LISBON

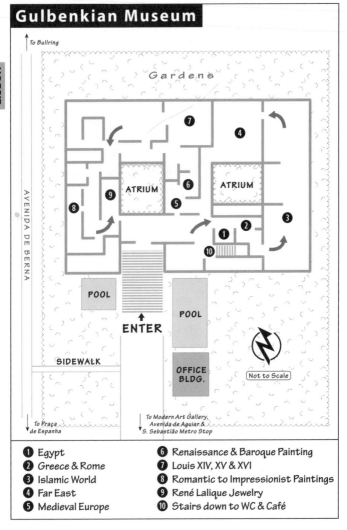

Gulbenkian Museum

To Bullring

Gardens

AVENIDA DE BERNA

7

4

6

9 ATRIUM ATRIUM

5

8

3

2

1

10

POOL

POOL

↑ ENTER

SIDEWALK

OFFICE BLDG.

N
Not to Scale

To Praça de Espanha

To Modern Art Gallery, Avenida de Aguiar & S. Sebastião Metro Stop

1 Egypt
2 Greece & Rome
3 Islamic World
4 Far East
5 Medieval Europe
6 Renaissance & Baroque Painting
7 Louis XIV, XV & XVI
8 Romantic to Impressionist Paintings
9 René Lalique Jewelry
10 Stairs down to WC & Café

wings, covering roughly pre-1500 and post-1500. Following the museum's layout, you'll see...

❶ Egypt (2,500-500 B.C.): Ancient Egyptians, believing that life really began after death, carved statues to preserve the memory of the deceased, whether it be a prince (Statue of the Courtier Bes, 664-610 B.C., with an inscription calling him "the king's friend") or a likeness of the family pet. The cat statue nurses her kittens atop a coffin that once held the cat's mummy, preserved for the afterlife. Egyptians honored cats—even giving them gold earrings like those on the statue. They believed cats helped the goddess

Bastet keep watch over the household. Now, more than 2,500 years later, we remember the Egyptians for these sturdy, dignified statues, built for eternity.

❷ Greece and Rome (500 B.C.-A.D. 500): The black-and-red Greek vase (calyx-crater), decorated with scenes of half-human satyrs chasing human women, reminds us of the rational Greeks' struggle to overcome their barbarian, animal-like urges as they invented Western civilization. Alexander the Great (r. 336-323 B.C., seen on a coin) used war to spread Greek culture throughout the Mediterranean, creating a cultural empire that would soon be taken over by Roman emperors (seen on medallions).

Journey even further back in time to the very roots of civilization: Mesopotamia (modern Iraq), where writing was invented. Five thousand years ago, the cylinder seals were used to roll an impression in sealing wax or clay.

❸ Islamic World (700-1500): The Muslims who lived in Portugal—as far west of Mecca as you could get back then—might have decorated their homes with furnishings from all over the Islamic world. Imagine a Moorish sultan, dressed in a shirt from Syria, sitting on a carpet from Persia in a courtyard with Moroccan tiles. By a bubbling fountain, he puffs on a hookah.

The culture of Moorish Iberia (711-1492) was among Europe's most sophisticated after the Fall of Rome. The intricate patterns on the glass lanterns are not only beautiful...they're actually quotes (in Arabic) from the Quran, such as "Allah (God) is the light of the world, shining like a flame in a glass lamp, as bright as a star."

❹ Far East (1368-1644): For almost 300 years, the Ming dynasty ruled China, having reclaimed the country from Genghis Khan and his sons. When Portuguese traders reached the Orient, they brought back blue-and-white ceramics such as these. They became all the rage, inspiring the creation of both Portuguese tiles and Dutch Delftware. Writing utensils fill elaborately decorated boxes from Japan. Another type of box was the ultimate picnic basket—*bento* was the best way to enjoy the Japanese countryside.

In the other wing, look for the art of...

❺ Medieval Europe (500-1500): While China was thriving and inventing, Europe was stuck in a thousand-year medieval funk (with the exception of Muslim Arab-ruled Iberia). Most Europeans from the "Age of Faith" channeled their spirituality into objects of Christian devotion. A priest on a business trip could pack a portable altarpiece in his backpack, travel to a remote village that had no church, and deliver a sermon carved in ivory. In monasteries, the monks with the best penmanship laboriously copied books (illuminated manuscripts) and decorated them with scenes from the text—and wacky doodles in the margins. These books were virtual time capsules, preserving the knowledge of Greece and Rome until it could emerge again, a thousand years later, in the Renaissance.

❻ **Renaissance and Baroque Painting (1500-1700):** Around 1500, a cultural revolution was taking place—the birth of humanism. Painters saw God in the faces of ordinary people, whether in Domenico Ghirlandaio's fresh-faced maiden, Frans Hals' wrinkled old woman, or Rembrandt's portrait of an old man, whose crease-lined hands tell the story of his life.

❼ **Louis XIV, XV, XVI (1700-1800):** After the Italian-born Renaissance, Europe's focus shifted northward to the luxurious court of France, where a new secular culture was blossoming. In one tapestry, love is in the air (see cupids flying overhead) as Venus frolics in a landscaped garden. Powder-wigged nobles in their palaces enjoyed the luxury of viewing art like this pagan scene, while relaxing in chairs like the kind you see here. This furniture, once owned by French kings (and Marie-Antoinette and Madame de Pompadour), is a royal home show. Anything heavy, ornate, and gilded (or that includes curved legs and animal-clawed feet) is from the time of Louis XIV. The Louis XV style is lighter and daintier, with Oriental motifs, while furniture from the Louis XVI era is stripped-down, straight-legged, tapered, and more modern. Listen to find out which clocks still work.

❽ **Romantic to Impressionist Paintings (1700-2000):** Europe ruled the world, and art became increasingly refined. Young British aristocrats (Thomas Gainsborough portrait) traveled Europe on the Grand Tour to see great sights like Venice (Guardi landscape). Follow the progression in styles from stormy Romanticism (J. M. W. Turner's tumultuous shipwreck) to Pre-Raphaelite dreamscapes *(Mirror of Venus)* to Realism's breath-of-fresh-air simplicity (Manet's bubble-blower) to the glinting, shimmering Impressionism of Monet... Renoir...and John Singer Sargent.

❾ **René Lalique Jewelry:** Finish your visit with the stunning, sumptuous Art Nouveau glasswork and jewelry of French designer René Lalique (1860-1945). Fragile beauty like this, from the elegant turn-of-the-century belle époque, was about to be shattered by the tumultuous 20th century. Art Nouveau emphasized forms from nature and valued the organic and artisan over cold, calculated mass production. Ordinary dragonflies, orchids, and beetles become breathtaking when transformed into jewelry. The work of Lalique—just another of Gulbenkian's circle of friends—is a fitting finale to a museum that features both history and beauty.

WEST LISBON
▲▲Museum of Ancient Art
(Museu Nacional de Arte Antiga)

This is Portugal's finest museum for paintings from its glory days, the 15th and 16th centuries. (Most of these works were gathered from Lisbon's abbeys and convents after their dissolution in 1834.) You'll also find a rich collection of furniture, as well as art by renowned European masters such as Hieronymus Bosch, Jan van Eyck, and Raphael—all in a grand palace. Pick up the free informative pamphlet at the entrance.

Cost and Hours: €6, free first Sun of every month; open Tue 14:00-18:00, Wed-Sun 10:00-18:00, closed Mon; tel. 213-912-800.

Getting There: It's about a mile west of downtown Lisbon at Rua das Janeles Verdes 9. From Praça da Figueira, take trolley #15E to Cais Rocha, cross the street, and walk up a lot of steps. Or take bus #714 from either Praça da Figueira or Praça do Comércio. The same bus and trolley continue to the sights in Belém.

Services: The museum has a good cafeteria with outdoor seating in a shaded garden overlooking the river.

Visiting the Museum: Here are some of the museum's highlights, starting on the top floor.

Third Floor—Portuguese Painting and Sculpture: The *Adoration of St. Vincent* in Room 12 is a multi-paneled altarpiece by the late-15th-century master Nuno Gonçalves. A gang of 60 real people—everyone from royalty to sailors and beggars—surrounds Lisbon's patron saint. Of note is the only recognized portrait of Prince Henry, responsible for setting Portugal on the path to exploration. Find him in the middle—an elder gentleman dressed in black with a wide-brimmed hat, hands together almost in prayer. In Room 3, if you've visited the sights in Belém, you'll recognize the Monastery of Jerónimos before it was fully

decorated (painting by Felipe Lobo in 1657). Find an exceptional portrait of young King Sebastian in Room 9. The armor is typical of Iberia for the era, as is the royal jaw and pursed lips due to Habsburg inbreeding. Considering Sebastian died so young, we are fortunate to have this wonderful portrait.

Second Floor—Japanese Screen and Jewels: Find the enchanting Namban screen paintings in Room 14 (*Namban* means "barbarians from the south"). It shows the Portuguese from a 16th-century Japanese perspective—with long noses as well as great skill at climbing rigging, like acrobats. The Portuguese, the first Europeans to make contact with Japan, gave the Japanese guns, Catholicism (Nagasaki was founded by Portuguese Jesuits), and a new deep-frying technique we now know as tempura.

On the same floor, have a quick look at the impressive jewelry collection decorated with the red cross of the Order of Christ, responsible for funding Portuguese explorations. Make your way to a freestanding glass case in Room 29 to see the Monstrance of Belém, made for Manuel I from the first gold brought back by Vasco da Gama. Restored in 2008, squint at the fine enamel creatures filling a tide pool on the base, the 12 apostles gathered around the glass case for the Communion wafer (the fancy top pops off), and the white dove hanging like a mobile under the all-powerful God bidding us peace on earth. Another notable monstrance is nearby in Room 27—a bejeweled Rococo masterpiece made for Lisbon's Bemposta Palace, with its carrying case displayed just behind it. More jewels and fine porcelain complete the rest of this floor; of note are tiles from Damascus—a gift from Calouste Gulbenkian. Before continuing downstairs, stop to admire a 17th-century painting of Lisbon before the 1755 earthquake.

First Floor—European Paintings: Pass through the gift shop and veer left (follow the numbering on the museum plan). Note the collection of the larger-than-life *Twelve Apostles* by the Spanish master Zurburán. Continue to the end of the hall, then go right into Room 61 for Bosch's *Temptations of St. Anthony* (a three-paneled altarpiece fantasy, c. 1500) and Albrecht Dürer's *St. Jerome*. St. Jerome is all-important to Lisbon as the primary figure behind the Monastery of Jerónimos in Belém. Finally, exit through the few remnants of the palace. Note the Pombal coat-of-arms that decorates the elaborate, Baroque doorway (find the star); the palace was originally purchased by the brother of the powerful Marquês de Pombal.

MODERN LISBON: ORIENTE, PARQUE DAS NAÇÕES, AND MORE

To get out of the quaint, Pombal-esque old town and enjoy a peek at the modern side of Lisbon, ride the Metro east to Oriente Station. Nearby you can stroll through a light and airy shopping mall, bike across the sprawling site of the 1998 World Expo, and promenade with locals along the Rio Tejo riverfront park. It's worth a visit any day, especially on Monday (when most museums in town are closed). It's a particularly vibrant scene when the people are out early on summer evenings.

Oriente Station (Gare do Oriente)

Oriente means "facing east." This impressive hub ties together trains (to the Algarve and Évora), the Metro, and buses under a swooping concrete roof designed by the Spanish architect Santiago Calatrava. From the Oriente Station, you'll notice right away that the theme here is the sea. That was the theme of the 1998 Expo. And just about everything in this area is named for the great Portuguese explorer Vasco da Gama.

Vasco da Gama Mall

Facing Oriente Station is the inviting, soaring glass facade of Lisbon's top shopping mall, also designed by Calatrava (daily 9:00-24:00). Originally the grand entrance to the 1998 World Expo, the city has done a good job of turning the remains of that fair into useful infrastructure. Stepping into the mall, you'll see that its design seems to have been inspired by the main shopping hall of a luxury cruise ship. Notice the water cascading down the glass roof—a clever and fun-to-look-at way to keep things cool and avoid any greenhouse effect. From the mall's entrance, climb the stairs to a small outdoor terrace for a good view back at the train station. Then stroll through the upper level of the mall to the opposite end, where you can step out to another outdoor terrace—giving you yet again the feeling that you're vacationing on a cruise ship. Survey the scene. With your back to the river, look up at the two skyscraping luxury condo buildings. With fine transportation connections and modern office space, this area holds lots of promise, both for residences and businesses. Microsoft set up its Portuguese headquarters here, and the Portuguese national court is in contemporary new buildings nearby. From here you can also look toward the river and survey Parque das Nações—the grounds of Portugal's 1998 World Expo (described next).

▲▲Parque das Nações

Lisbon celebrated the 500th anniversary of Vasco da Gama's voyage to India by hosting Expo '98 here at Parque das Nações. The theme was "The Ocean and the Seas," emphasizing the global importance of healthy, clean waters.

To get the lay of the land, climb to the outdoor terrace at the Vasco de Gama Mall (see previous listing), or look out over the Grand Esplanade (Rossio Olivais). Ahead of you, lining the espla-

LISBON

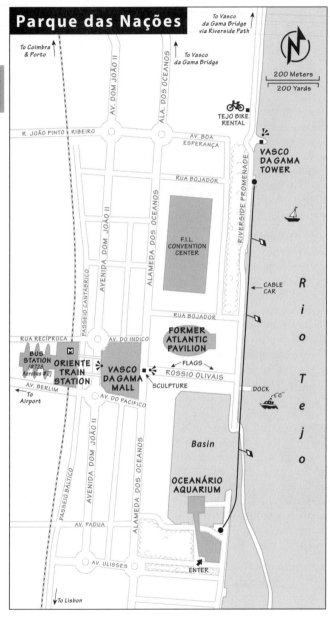

Parque das Nações

To Coimbra & Porto

To Vasco da Gama Bridge via Riverside Path

To Vasco da Gama Bridge

200 Meters
200 Yards

AV. DOM JOÃO II

ALA. DOS OCEANOS

R. JOÃO PINTO RIBEIRO

AV. BOA ESPERANÇA

RUA BOJADOR

TEJO BIKE RENTAL

VASCO DA GAMA TOWER

RIVERSIDE PROMENADE

AVENIDA DOM JOÃO II

ALAMEDA DOS OCEANOS

F.I.L. CONVENTION CENTER

PASSEIO CANTÁBRICO

RUA RECÍPROCA

AV. DO INDICO

BUS STATION (#728, Aerobus #2)

ORIENTE TRAIN STATION

VASCO DA GAMA MALL

AV. BERLIM

To Airport

AV. DO PACIFICO

RUA BOJADOR

FORMER ATLANTIC PAVILION

FLAGS

ROSSIO OLIVAIS

SCULPTURE

CABLE CAR

DOCK

R i o   T e j o

AVENIDA DOM JOÃO II

ALAMEDA DOS OCEANOS

PASSEIO BÁLTICO

Basin

OCEANÁRIO AQUARIUM

AV. PADUA

AV. ULISSES

ENTER

To Lisbon

nade, are 155 flags—one for each country represented at the fair. The flags are arranged in alphabetical order, so the first ones are South Africa (Africa dul Sul), Albania, and Germany (Alemanha). In the middle you'll find the US (Estados Unidos), Spain (Espanha), and Estonia side by side. The striped oval dome to the left, once the Atlantic Pavilion (Pavilhão Atlântico), is now an 18,000-seat concert hall. The oil refinery tower far to the right marks the west end of the park and stands as a reminder of the industrial wasteland that was here before the fair.

The basin in front of you pre-dates the fair. Back before World War II it was a watery "parking lot" (just 1.5 yards deep) for seaplanes. Across the basin to your right, the blocky building that resembles an aircraft carrier with a spiky rooftop is the Oceanário aquarium (described later)—the big hit of the fair and still the park's major attraction. From behind that the cable car (€4

one-way, €6 round-trip, nothing special) drifts east to the Vasco da Gama Tower, which marks that end of the park. Two miles away, built as part of the 1998 celebrations, is the Vasco da Gama Bridge (described later). A delightful promenade (Caminho dos Pinheiros; "The Way of the Pine Trees") runs along the riverfront from the marina all the way to a park at the base of the Vasco de Gama Bridge.

Parque das Nações Bike Ride

The most enjoyable way to explore the sprawling park is by bike. Simply enjoy a big loop pedaling around modern art, under fancy eaves, along the riverside promenade, and past local lovers enjoying a little *"marmalade"* (local slang for heavy petting). **Tejo Bike Rental,** which operates out of a red shipping container on the Grand Esplanade (*Esplanando,* north of the Vasco da Gama Tower), rents simple one-speed bikes (€3/30 minutes, €5/hour, daily in summer 10:00-20:00, off-season 12:00-18:00, no locks).

Oceanário

Europe's largest aquarium simulates four different oceanic underwater and shoreline environments. Built in a modern version of a ship at sea, the aquarium's enormous centerpiece is a central tank with lots of fish and the occasional hungry shark. Penguins, sea otters, and weekday-morning school groups are all happily on display.

Cost and Hours: €16, daily April-Oct 10:00-20:00, off-season until 19:00, last entry one hour before closing, tel. 218-917-000, www.oceanario.pt.

Azulejos

During visits to neighboring Spain, King Manuel I not only acquired wives, but he also obtained several thousand tiles to decorate palaces throughout Portugal. Vibrant colors must have attracted the king's attention, and some examples from his visits can still be seen in the National Palace in Sintra. It wasn't long before Portuguese artists began producing for local clients, and tiles became synonymous with the seafaring empire.

The biggest challenge for early artisans was how to keep colors separate during the firing process. A number of techniques developed to solve this problem: *Alicatados* are mosaic pieces, cut after firing, to form intricate geometric patterns; *corda seca* fills thick outlines of manganese oxide with different colors, like a children's coloring book; and *aresta* sculpts color wells directly into the tile. The biggest breakthrough came with the development of *majólica*, or *faiança*—the undecorated clay tile is baked first, then covered with an opaque glaze that makes a canvas for the painted design, which is set by a second firing.

Brazilians loved tilework, too, and after the return of the Portuguese king to European shores, factories began producing tilework for the masses. But tilework began to fall out of fashion by the early 20th century. Then Lisbon's 1959 Metro system gave tile artists a new playground. While not originally in the budget, artist Maria Keil could not bear to see the walls vacant. Her original designs are still on display, and future artists continue to make the Metro an underground art museum.

Unfortunately, others have noticed the beauty (and profitability) of historic tilework panels. Theft is common—often for resale on the black market—and many of Lisbon's older panels are at risk. In the past decade, local watch groups have documented several hundred cases of missing panels and helped recover several of them. Think twice before purchasing tilework at the Feira da Ladra flea market.

To go on your own *azulejo* scavenger hunt, check out Endless Mile's tile guide to Lisbon that lists nearly 100 of the city's best tile panels (www.endlessmile.com).

Vasco da Gama Bridge

Europe's longest bridge (10.7 miles) was opened in 1998 to connect the Expo grounds with the south side of the Rio Tejo, and to alleviate the traffic jams on Lisbon's only other bridge over the river, the 25th of April Bridge. The Vasco de Gama Bridge helped connect north and south Portugal, back when a freeway was a big deal in this late-to-develop European nation. Built low to the water, the bridge's towers and cables are meant to suggest the sails of a caravel ship.

EAST LISBON
▲National Tile Museum (Museu Nacional do Azulejo)

Filling the Convento da Madre de Deus, the museum features piles of tiles, which, as you've probably noticed, are an art form in Portu-

gal. They've tried to show-
case the tiles as they would
have originally appeared
(note the diamond-shaped
staircase tiles). While the
presentation is low-tech,
the church is sumptuous,
and the tile panorama
of pre-earthquake Lisbon
(upstairs) is fascinating.

Cost and Hours: €5, free first Sun of every month; open Tue-Sun 10:00-18:00, closed Mon; last entry 30 minutes before closing; located about a mile east of Praça do Comércio—15 minutes on bus #794 from Praça do Comércio or bus #742 from São Sebastião Metro station (near Gulbenkian Museum), buses stop at museum entrance on Rua da Madre de Deus 4, tel. 218-100-340, mnazulejo. imc-ip.pt.

SOUTH OF LISBON, ACROSS THE RIVER
▲25th of April Bridge (25 de Abril)

At 1.5 miles (3,280 feet between the towers), this is one of the longest suspension bridges in the world. The foundations are sunk

260 feet below the surface into the riverbed, making it the world's deepest bridge. It was built in 1966 by the same company that made its famous San Francisco cousin (but notice the lower deck for train tracks). Originally named for the dictator Salazar, the bridge was renamed for the date of Portugal's 1974 revolution and liberation. For a generation, natives would show their political colors by choosing which name to use. While conser-

vative Portuguese called it the "Salazar Bridge," liberals referred to it as the "25th of April Bridge" (just as Washington, D.C.'s airport is called "National" by some and "Reagan" by others). Imagine that before 1966, there was no way across the Rio Tejo except by ferry.

António Salazar

Q: What do you get when you cross a lawyer, an economist, and a dictator?

A: António Salazar, who was all three—a dictator who ruled Portugal through harsh laws and a strict budget that hurt the poor.

Shortly after a 1926 military coup "saved" Portugal's floundering democracy from itself, General Oscar Carmona appointed António de Oliveira Salazar (1889-1970) as finance minister. A former professor of economics and law at the University of Coimbra, Salazar balanced the budget and the interests of the country's often-warring factions. His skill and his reputation as a clean-living, fair-minded patriot earned him a promotion. In 1932, he became prime minister, and he set about creating his New State *(Estado Novo)*.

For nearly four decades, Salazar ruled a stable but isolated nation based on harmony between the traditional power blocs of the ruling class—the military, big business, large landowners, and the Catholic Church. This Christian fascism, backed by the military and secret police, was ratified repeatedly in elections by the country's voters—the richest 20 percent of the populace.

As a person, Salazar was respected, but not loved. The son of a farm manager, he originally studied to be a priest before going on to become a scholar and writer. He never married. Quiet, low-key, and unassuming, he attended church regularly and lived a nonmaterialistic existence. But when faced with opposition, he was ruthless, and his secret police became an object of fear and hatred.

Salazar steered Portugal through the turmoil of Spain's Civil War (1936-1939), remaining officially neutral while secretly supporting Franco's fascists. He detested Nazi Germany's "pagan" leaders, but respected Mussolini for reconciling with the pope. In World War II, Portugal was officially neutral, but was often friendly with longtime ally Britain and used as a base for espionage. After the war, it benefited greatly from the United States' Marshall Plan for economic recovery (which Spain missed out on during Franco's rule), and the country joined NATO in 1949.

Salazar distracted his poor and isolated masses with a cynical credo: *"Fado, Fátima, and Futebol"* (the three "Fs"). Salazar's regime was undone by two factors: the liberal 1960s and the unpopular, draining wars Portugal fought abroad to try to keep its colonial empire intact. When Salazar died in 1970, the regime that followed became increasingly less credible, leading to the liberating events of the Carnation Revolution in 1974.

LISBON

Cristo Rei (Christ of Majesty)

A huge, 330-foot concrete statue of Christ (à la Rio de Janeiro, in the former Portuguese colony of Brazil) overlooks Lisbon from across

the Rio Tejo, stretching its arms wide to symbolically bless the city (or as less reverent Portuguese say, "to dive into the river"). Lisbon's cardinal, inspired by a visit to Rio de Janeiro in 1936, wanted a replica built back home. Increased support came after an appeal was made to Our Lady of Fátima in 1940 to keep Portugal out of World War II. Portugal survived the war relatively unscathed, and funds were collected to build this statue in appreciation. After 10 years of construction, it opened to the public in 1959. It's now a sanctuary and pilgrimage site, and the chapel inside holds regular Sunday Mass. The statue was designed to be seen from a distance, and there's little reason to go to the trouble of actually visiting it. If you do visit, an elevator will take you to the top for a panoramic view: From left to right, see Belém, the 25th of April Bridge, downtown Lisbon (Praça do Comércio and the green Alfama hilltop with the castle), and the long Vasco da Gama Bridge.

Cost and Hours: €5, daily 9:30-18:00, until 19:00 in summer, last elevator ride 15 minutes before closing, tel. 212-751-000.

Getting There: To get to Cristo Rei, catch the 10-minute ferry from downtown Lisbon to Cacilhas (€2, 4/hour, more during rush hour, from Cais do Sodré Metro/train station follow signs to *Terminal Fluvial*, which serves many destinations). The bus marked *101 Cristo Rei* takes you to the base of the statue in 15 minutes (3/hour, exit ferry dock left into the maze of bus stops to find the #20 stop with the "101 Cristo Rei" schedule under the awning). Because of bridge tolls to enter Lisbon, taxis from the site are expensive. Consider taking a late-morning ferry to Cristo Rei; catch a taxi from the statue to Porto Brandão and have lunch there; and ferry direct to Belém and see the sights. For drivers, the most efficient visit is a quick stop on your way to or from Évora or the Algarve.

BELÉM

Three miles west of downtown Lisbon, the Belém district is a stately pincushion of important sights from Portugal's Golden Age, when Vasco da Gama and company turned the country into Europe's richest power. Belém was the send-off point for voyages in the Age of Discovery. Sailors would stay and pray here before embarking. The tower welcomed them home. The grand buildings of Belém survived the great 1755 earthquake, so this is the best

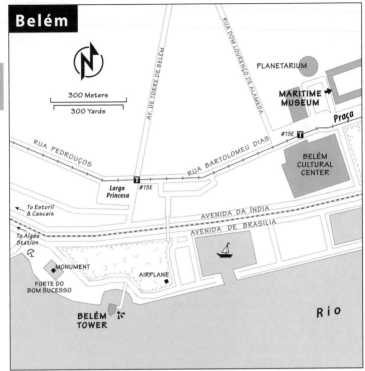

place to experience the grandeur of pre-earthquake Lisbon. After the earthquake, safety-conscious (and rattled) royalty chose to live here—in wooden rather than stone buildings. The modern-day president of Portugal calls Belém home.

To celebrate the 300th anniversary of independence from Spain, a grand exhibition was held here in 1940, resulting in the fine parks, fountains, and monuments. Nearly all of Belém's museums are closed on Monday (though the Monument to the Discoveries is open Mon May-Sept).

Getting to Belém

You'll get here quickest by taxi (€15 from downtown). Buses #714 and #728 serve Belém, but I prefer riding the slower trolley #15E (30-40 minutes, catch at Praça da Figueira or Praça do Comércio). In Belém, the first trolley stop is at the National Coach Museum, the second is at the Monastery of Jerónimos, and another is two blocks inland from the Belém Tower. Even if you miss the first stop, you can't miss the second stop at the massive monastery.

Consider doing Belém in this order: the National Coach Museum, pastry and coffee break, Monastery of Jerónimos, Maritime

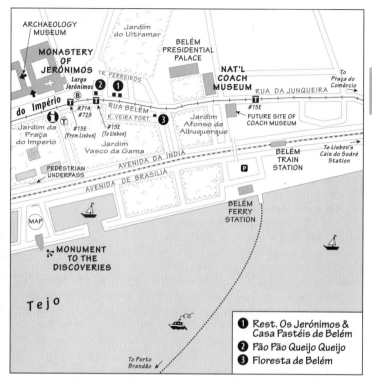

ARCHAEOLOGY MUSEUM

Jardim do Ultramar

MONASTERY OF JERÓNIMOS

BELÉM PRESIDENTIAL PALACE

NAT'L COACH MUSEUM

TR. FERREIROS

Largo Jerónimos

do Império

RUA DA JUNQUEIRA

To Praça do Comércio

RUA BELÉM

R. VEIRA PORT.

#714, #728

#15E (From Lisbon)

#15E (To Lisbon)

Jardim da Praça do Imperio

Jardim Afonso de Albuquerque

FUTURE SITE OF COACH MUSEUM

#15E

Jardim Vasco da Gama

AVENIDA DA INDIA

BELÉM TRAIN STATION

To Lisbon's Cais do Sodré Station

PEDESTRIAN UNDERPASS

AVENIDA DE BRASILIA

MAP

BELÉM FERRY STATION

MONUMENT TO THE DISCOVERIES

Tejo

To Porto Brandão

❶ Rest. Os Jerónimos & Casa Pastéis de Belém
❷ Pão Pão Queijo Queijo
❸ Floresta de Belém

Museum (if interested) and/or lunch at its cafeteria (public access, museum entry not required), Monument to the Discoveries, and Belém Tower. If arriving by taxi, start at Belém Tower, the far-thest point, and do the recommended lineup in reverse, ending at the National Coach Museum. Belém also has a cultural center, a children's museum, and a planetarium—not priorities for a quick visit.

When you're through, hop on trolley #15E or bus #714 to re-turn to Praça da Figueira or Praça do Comércio. Bus #728 takes you to Santa Apolónia Station, and continues to Parque das Nações and Oriente Station.

Tourist Information

The little TI kiosk is directly across the street from the entrance to the monastery (Tue-Sat 10:00-13:00 & 14:00-18:00, closed Sun-Mon, tel. 213-658-437).

A little **Yellow Bus Tour** minibus offers a handy hop-on, hop-off tour around the Belém sights—which can feel far-flung if you're tired—departing every hour from the monastery entrance. You can get off to explore a sight and catch the next minibus (€5, daily, departs every 30 minutes, June-Sept 10:00-13:00 & 14:00-18:30).

Between the Coach Museum and Monastery
▲▲National Coach Museum

In 1905, the last Queen of Portugal saw that cars would soon obliterate horse-drawn carriages as a form of transportation. She decided to use the palace's riding-school building to preserve her fine collection of royal coaches, which became today's National Coach Museum (Museu dos Coches). A new, larger museum is being built kitty-corner from the present location. The following description is based on the current configuration; if you visit after the new building opens, request a map as you enter.

Cost and Hours: €6, free first Sun of every month, Tue-Sun 10:00-18:00, closed Mon, last entry 30 minutes before closing, tel. 213-610-850, www.museudoscoches.pt.

Visiting the Museum: The collection is impressive, with more than 70 dazzling carriages (described in English) lining the elegant old riding room. Check out the ceiling, which is as remarkable as the carriages, and look for coach #1 (from around 1600). This crude and simple coach was once used by Philip II, king of Spain and Portugal, to shuttle between Madrid and Lisbon. Notice that the coach has no driver's seat—its drivers would actually ride the horses. You'll have to trust me on this, but if you lift up the cushion from the passengers' seat, you'll find a potty hole—also handy for road sickness. Imagine how slow and rough the ride would be with bad roads and a crude leather-strap suspension.

Study the evolution of suspension technology, starting with the first coach, or "Kotze," made in the 15th century in a Hungarian town of that name. Trace the improvement of coaches through the next century, noticing that as the decoration increases, so does the comfort. A Portuguese coat of arms indicates that a carriage was part of the royal fleet. Ornamentation often includes a folk festival of exotic faces from Portugal's distant colonies. Examples of period riding costumes are displayed in cases between many of the coaches.

At the far end of the first room, the lumbering Ocean Coach, as ornate as it is long, stands shining. At the stern, gold figures symbolize the Atlantic and Indian Oceans holding hands, a reminder of Portugal's mastery of the sea. The Ocean Coach is flanked by two equally stunning coaches with similar symbols of ocean exploration.

The second room shows sedan chairs and traces the development of carriages as a common means of transportation. They got lighter and faster, culminating in a sporty, horse-drawn Lisbon

Wander upstairs to get a glimpse of velvet-covered saddles and special riding gear designed for the royal kids. A spectacular view of the entire building interior is picture-perfect (no flash). The portrait gallery of most Portuguese royalty is handy for putting a face to all the movers and shakers you've read about so far.

▲Casa Pastéis de Belém

The Casa Pastéis de Belém café is the birthplace of the wonderful custard tart that's called *pastel de nata* throughout Portugal, but here is dubbed *pastel de Belém*. Since 1837, residents have come to this café to get their tarts warm out of the oven. This place's popularity stems mainly from the fact that their recipe is a closely guarded secret—supposedly only three people know the exact proportions of ingredients. While the recipe is fine, my hunch is that the explanation for their undeniable goodness is simply that, because they crank out 20,000 or so a day, you get them fresh and crunchy, literally hot out of the oven. (Take one back to your hotel and eat it tonight and it'll taste just like any other in town.) Sit down and enjoy one with a *café com leite*. Sprinkle on as much cinnamon and powdered sugar as you like. If the to-go line is too long, there's plenty of seating in the café and perhaps faster service (if you need a WC, this is an easy choice). You can also often save time by lining up not at the front counter but on the back side of the counter (tarts €1.05 each, daily 8:00-24:00, Rua de Belém 84, tel. 213-637-423).

▲▲▲Monastery of Jerónimos

King Manuel (who ruled from 1495) erected this giant, white limestone church and monastery—which stretches 300 yards

along the Lisbon waterfront—as a "thank you" for the discoveries made by early Portuguese explorers. It was financed in part with "pepper money," a 5 percent tax on spices brought back from India. Manuel built the church on the site of a humble chapel where sailors spent their last night ashore in prayer before embarking on frightening voyages. What is the style of Manuel's church? Manueline.

Cost and Hours: The church is free, but the cloister costs €10. A €12 combo-ticket saves you €2 if you also visit the Tower of Belém (both the cloister and tower are free on first Sun of every month; hours for monastery: May-Sept Tue-Sun 10:00-18:30, off-season until 17:30, closed Mon, last entry 30 minutes before closing, www.mosteirojeronimos.pt; can purchase tickets online at bilhetes.igespar.pt). There's often a long line to visit the cloister, but you can cut through it to get to the church entrance.

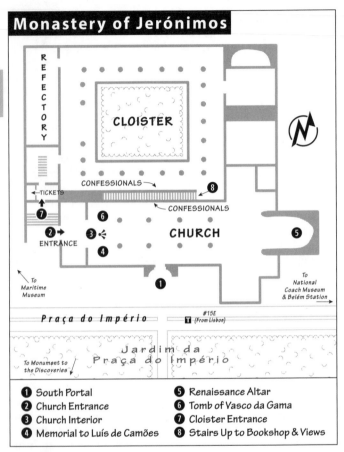

Monastery of Jerónimos

- ❶ South Portal
- ❷ Church Entrance
- ❸ Church Interior
- ❹ Memorial to Luís de Camões
- ❺ Renaissance Altar
- ❻ Tomb of Vasco da Gama
- ❼ Cloister Entrance
- ❽ Stairs Up to Bookshop & Views

⊙ **Self-Guided Tour:** Here's a tour, starting outside the monastery:

❶ **South Portal:** The fancy portal, facing the street, is textbook Manueline. Henry the Navigator stands between the doors with the king's patron saint, St. Jerome (above on the left, with the lion). Henry (Manuel's uncle) built the original sailors' chapel on this site. This door is only used when Mass lets out or for Saturday weddings. (The electronic snapping sound you hear is designed to keep the pigeons away.)

❷ **Church Entrance:** As you approach the main entrance, the church is on your right and the cloister is straight ahead. Flanking the church door are kneeling statues of King Manuel I, the Fortunate (left of door, with St. Jerome), and his Spanish wife, María (right, with John the Baptist).

❸ **Church Interior:** The Manueline style is on the cusp of

the Renaissance. The space is more open than earlier medieval churches. Slender, palm tree-like columns don't break the interior space (as Gothic columns would), and the ceiling is all one height. Motifs from the sea hide in the decor. The sea brought Portugal 16th-century wealth and power, making this art possible. You'll see rope-like arches, ships, and monsters that evoke the mystery of undiscovered lands. Artichokes, eaten for their vitamin C to fend off scurvy, remind us of the hardships sailors faced at sea.

❹ Memorial to Luís de Camões: Camões (kah-MOISH, 1524-1580) is Portugal's Shakespeare and Casanova rolled into one, an adventurer and writer whose heroic poems glorifying the nation's sailing exploits live on today. It was Camões who described Portugal as the place "where land ends and the sea begins."

After college at Coimbra, Camões was banished from the court (1546) for flirting with the noble lady Dona Caterina. He lost an eye soldiering in Morocco (he's always portrayed squinting), served jail time for brawling with a bureaucrat, and then caught a ship to India and China, surviving a shipwreck on the way. While serving as a colonial administrator in India, he plugged away at the epic poem that would become his masterpiece. Returning to Portugal, he published *The Lusiads* (*Os Lusíadas*, 1572), winning minor recognition and a small pension.

The long poem describes Vasco da Gama's first voyage to India in heroic terms, on the scale of Homer's *Odyssey*. *The Lusiads* begins:

> *Arms and the heroes, from Lisbon's shore,*
> *sailed through seas never dared before,*
> *with awesome courage, forging their way*
> *to the glorious kingdoms of the rising day.*

The poem goes on to recite many events in Portuguese history, from the time of the Lusiads (the original pre-Roman natives) onward. Even today, Camões' words are quoted by modern Portuguese politicians in search of a heroic sound bite. And Portugal's national holiday, June 10, is known as Camões Day, remembering the day in 1580 when the great poet died. The stone monument here—with literary rather than maritime motifs—is a cenotaph (his actual burial spot is unknown).

❺ Renaissance Altar: Nearly everything here survived the 1755 earthquake, except for the stained glass (the replacement glass is from 1940). In the main altar, elephants—the Oriental symbol of power, which dethroned lions as the most powerful and kingly of beasts—support two kings and two queens (King Manuel I is front-left). Many Portuguese churches (such as the cathedrals in downtown Lisbon and Évora) were renovated in Renaissance and Baroque times, resulting in an odd mix of dark, older naves and pretty pastel altars. Walk back on the side with the seven wooden confessional doors (on your right). Notice the ornamental carving around the second one: a festival of faces from newly discovered corners of the world. Head back toward the entry. Under a ceiling that's a veritable *Boy Scout's Handbook* of rope and knots) is the...

❻ Tomb of Vasco da Gama: On the night of July 7, 1497, in the small chapel that stood here before the current church was

built, da Gama (1460-1524) prayed for a safe voyage. The next day, he set sail from Belém with four ships (see the caravel carved in the middle of the tomb's side) and 150 men. He was armed with state-of-the-art maps and sailing technology, such as the carved armillary sphere, a globe surrounded by movable rings designed to determine the positions of the sun or other stars to help sailors track their location on earth. (Some say its diagonal slash is symbolic of the unwritten pact and ambition of Spain and Portugal to split the world evenly, but it actually represents the path of the planets as they move across the heavens.)

Da Gama's mission? To confirm what earlier navigators had hypothesized—that the ocean recently discovered when Bartolomeu Dias rounded Africa was the same one seen by overland travelers to India. Hopefully, da Gama would find a direct sea route to the vast, untapped wealth of Asia. The symbols on the tomb show the icons of the period—the cross (symbolizing the religious military order of the soldier monks who funded these voyages), the caravel (representing the method of travel), and Portugal's trading power around the globe (the result).

By Christmas, da Gama rounded the Cape of Good Hope. After battling hostile Arabs in Mozambique, he hired an Arab guide to pilot the ships to India, arriving on the southwest coast in Calicut (from which we get the word "calico") in May of 1498. He traded for spices, networked with the locals for future outposts, battled belligerent chiefs, and then headed back home. Da Gama and his crew arrived home to Lisbon in September of 1499 (after two years and two months on the seas) and were greeted with all-out Vasco-mania. The few spices he'd returned with (many were lost in transit) were worth a staggering fortune. Portugal's Golden Age was launched.

Manueline Architecture
(c. 1480-1580)

Portugal's unique style (from its peak of power under King Manuel I, the Fortunate, r. 1495-1521) reflects the wealth of the

times and the many cultural influences of the Age of Discovery. The purpose is decorative, not structural. Whether the building uses pointed Gothic or round Renaissance arches, it can be embellished with elaborate Manueline carved stonework, particularly around windows and doors.

Manueline aesthetic is ornate, elaborate, and intertwined, often featuring symbols from a family's coat of arms (shields with castles, crosses, lions, banners, and crowns) or motifs from the sea (rope-like columns or borders, knots, shells, coral, anchors, and nets). Manuel's personal symbol was the armillary sphere—a globe of the earth surrounded by movable rings—which was an indispensable navigational aid for sailors. You'll also see imports of the age, from opium poppies to strange animals.

Architecture students will recognize elements from Gothic's elaborate tracery, the abstract designs of Moorish culture, similarities to Spain's intricate Plateresque style (which dates from the same time), and the elongated excesses of Italian Mannerism.

King Manuel dubbed da Gama "Admiral of the Sea of India" and sent him out again, this time to subdue the Indian people, establish more trade outposts, and again return home to wealth and honor. Da Gama died on Christmas Eve 1524, in India. His memory lives on due to the tribute of two men: Manuel, who built this large church, and Luís de Camões (honored opposite Vasco), who turned da Gama's history-making voyage into an epic poem.

❼ Cloister: Leave the church (turn right), purchase your ticket, and enter the cloister. The restored cloister is the architectural highlight of Belém. The lacy arcade is Manueline; the simpler diamond and decorative rose frieze above the top floor is Renaissance. Study the carvings, especially the gargoyles above the lower set of arches. Among these functioning rainspouts, find a monkey, a kitten, and a cricket. The small basin in the corner (where the monks

LISBON

washed up before meals) marks the entrance to the refectory, or dining hall—today an occasional concert venue lined with fine 18th-century tiles. The tiles are considered textbook Rococo (from the French word for "shell," as you can see). Rococo ignores the parameters set by the architecture, unlike Baroque, which works within the structure.

To the left of the refectory is the burial spot of Portugal's most revered modern poet, Fernando Pessoa. Continuing around, a large room contains an exhibit of the lengthy restoration process, as well as the tomb of Alexandre Herculano, a Romantic 19th-century historian and poet. Quotes from Herculano adorn his tomb: "Sleep? Only the cold cadaver that doesn't feel sleeps. The soul flies and wraps itself around the feet of the All-Powerful."

Heads of state are often received in the cloister with a warm welcome. This is also the site of many important treaty signings, such as Portugal's admittance to the European Union in 1986.

❽ **Upstairs:** You'll find a bookshop, WCs (women's downstairs, men's upstairs), and better views of the church and the cloister, along with exhibits about the monastery's history.

Monks often accompanied the sailor-pirates on their trading/pillaging trips, hoping to convert the heathens to Christianity. Many expeditions were financed by the Knights of Christ, a brotherhood of soldier monks. (The monks who inhabited this cloister were Hieronymites—followers of St. Jerome, hence the monastery name of Jerónimos.)

King Manuel, who did so much to promote exploration, was also the man who forcibly expelled all Jews from the country. (In 1497, the Spanish *Reyes Católicos*—Ferdinand and Isabel—agreed to allow him to marry one of their daughters on the condition that he deport the Jews.) Francis Xavier, a Spanish Jesuit, did much of his missionary work traveling in Asia in the service of Portugal.

It was a time of extreme Christian faith. The sheer size of this religious complex is a testament to the zealous motivation that—along with money—propelled the Age of Discovery.

Age of Discovery Sights
▲Maritime Museum (Museu de Marinha)

If you're interested in Portugal's historic ships and navigational tools, this museum, which fills the west wing of the Monastery of Jerónimos (listed earlier) and has good English descriptions, is worth a look. Sailors love it.

Cost and Hours: €5, free Sun 10:00-14:00; open daily May-Sept 10:00-18:00, off-season until 17:00; facing the planetarium from the square, a cafeteria—open to the public—is to your left and the museum entrance is to your right.

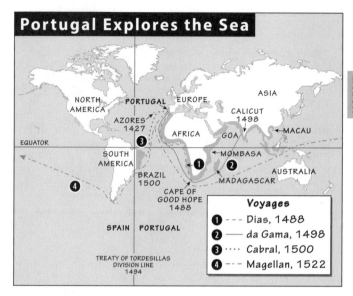

Portugal Explores the Sea

Voyages

1 - - - Dias, 1488
2 —— da Gama, 1498
3 ···· Cabral, 1500
4 - – - Magellan, 1522

▲Monument to the Discoveries
(Padrão dos Descobrimentos)

In 1960, the city honored the 500th anniversary of the death of Prince Henry the Navigator by rebuilding this giant riverside mon-

ument, which had originally been constructed for the 1940 World Expo (reached from the monastery via a pedestrian tunnel under the busy boulevard). The elevator inside takes you up to a tingly view.

Cost and Hours: €3; May-Sept daily 10:00-19:00; Oct-April Tue-Sun 10:00-18:00, closed Mon; last entry 30 minutes before closing, tel. 213-031-950.

Visiting the Monument: Walk around the huge monument. The 170-foot concrete structure shows that exploring the world was a team effort. The men who braved the unknown stand on the pointed, raised prow of a caravel, about to be launched into the Rio Tejo.

Leading the charge is Prince Henry the Navigator, holding a model of a caravel and a map, followed by kneeling kings and soldiers who Christianized foreign lands with the sword. Behind Henry (on the west side, away from bridge), find the men who financed the voyages (King Manuel I, holding an armillary sphere, his personal symbol), those who glorified it in poems and paintings (like Luís de Camões, holding his famous poem *Os Lusíadas* on a

Caravels

These easily maneuverable trading ships were fast, small (80 feet), and light (100 tons), with few guns and three triangular-shaped sails (called lateen-rigged sails) that could pivot quickly to catch the wind. They were ideal for sailing along coastlines. Many oceangoing caravels were also rigged with a square foresail to make them more stable. (This photo shows the model held by Prince Henry on Belém's Monument to the Discoveries.) Columbus' *Niña* and *Pinta* were re-rigged caravels.

scroll), and at the very end, the only woman, Philippa of Lancaster, Henry's British mother.

On the east side (closest to bridge—as you walk, notice the optical illusion of waves on the flat cobbled surface), Vasco da Gama stands with his eyes on the horizon and his hand on his sword. Magellan holds a circle, representing the round earth his ship circumnavigated, while in front of him, Pedro Cabral puts his hand to his heart, thankful to have (perhaps accidentally) discovered Brazil. Various monks, navigators with maps, and crusaders with flags complete the crew. Check out the pillory, decorated with the Portuguese coat of arms and a cross, erected in each place discovered by the Portuguese—leaving no doubt as to who was in charge.

In the **marble map in the pavement** (a gift from South Africa) in front of the Monument to the Discoveries, follow Portugal's explorers as they inched out into monster-infested waters at the edge of the world. From their tiny, isolated nation in Europe, the Portuguese first headed south to the coast of Morocco, conquering the Muslims of Ceuta in God's name (1415), and gaining strategic control of the mouth of the Mediterranean. They braved the open Atlantic to the west and southwest, stumbling on the Madeiras (1420), which Prince Henry planted with vineyards, and the remote Azore Islands (1427).

Meanwhile, the Portuguese slowly moved southward, hugging the African coast, each voyage building on the knowledge from previous expeditions. They cleared the biggest psychological hump when Gil Eanes sailed around Cape Bojador (Western Sahara, 1434)—the border of the known world—and into the equatorial seas where it was thought that sea monsters lurked, no winds blew, and ships would be incinerated in the hot sun. Eanes survived, returning home with 200 Africans in chains, the first of what would

The Age of Discovery

In 1560, you could sail from Lisbon to China without ever losing sight of land explored by Portugal. The riches of the  world poured into the tiny nation—spices from India and Java (black pepper, cinnamon, and curry powder); ivory, diamonds, and slaves (sold to New World plantations) from Africa; sugarcane, gold, and diamonds from Brazil; and, from everywhere, knowledge of new plants, animals, and customs. How did tiny Portugal pull this off?

First, its people were motivated by greed, hoping to break the Arab and Venetian monopoly on Eastern luxury goods (the price of pepper was jacked up 1,000 percent by the time it reached European dinner tables). They were also driven by a crusading Christian spirit, a love of science, and a spirit of adventure. An entire 15th-century generation was obsessed with finding the legendary kingdom of the fabulously wealthy Christian named "Prester John," supposedly located in either India or Africa. (The legend may be based on a historical figure from around 1120 who visited the pope in Rome as "patriarch of India.")

Portugal also had certain natural advantages. Its Atlantic location led to a strong maritime tradition. A unified nation-state (one of Europe's first) financed and coordinated expeditions. And a core of technology-savvy men used and developed their expansive knowledge of navigational devices, astronomy, maps, shipbuilding, and languages.

become a lucrative, abhorrent commodity. Two generations later, Bartolomeu Dias rounded the southern tip of Africa (1488), discovering the sea route to Asia that Vasco da Gama (1498) and others would exploit to colonize India, Indonesia, Japan, and China (Macao in 1557, on the south coast).

In 1500, Pedro Cabral (along with Dias and 1,200 men) took a wi-i-i-ide right turn on the way down the African coast, hoping to avoid windless seas, and landed on the tip of Brazil. Brazil proved to be an agricultural goldmine for Portugal, which profited from sugar plantations worked by African slaves. Two hundred years later, gold and gemstones were discovered in Brazil, jumpstarting the Portuguese economy again.

In 1520, Portuguese Ferdinand Magellan, employed by Spain, sailed west with five ships and 270 men, broke for R&R in Rio, continued through the Straits of Magellan (tip of South America), and suffered through mutinies, scurvy, and dinners of sawdust and ship rats before touching land in Guam. Magellan was killed in battle in the Philippines, but one remaining ship continued west and arrived back in Europe, having circumnavigated the globe after 30 months at sea.

By 1560, Portugal's global empire had peaked. Tiny-but-filthy-rich Portugal claimed (though they didn't actually occupy) the entire coastline of Africa, Arabia, India, the Philippines, and south China—a continuous stretch from Lisbon to Macao—plus Brazil. The Treaty of Tordesillas (1494) with Spain divvied up the colonial world between the two nations, split at 45 degrees west longitude (bisecting South America—and explaining why Brazil speaks Portuguese and the rest of the continent speaks Spanish) and 135 degrees east longitude (bisecting the Philippines and Australia).

But all of the wealth was wasted on Portugal's ruling class, who neglected to reinvest it in the future. Easy money ruined the traditional economy and stunted industry, hurting the poor. Over the next four centuries, one by one, Portugal's colonies were lost to other European nations or to local revolutions. Today, only the (largely autonomous) islands of the Azores and Madeiras remain from the once-global empire.

▲Belém Tower

Perhaps the purest Manueline building in Portugal (built 1515-1520), this white tower protected Lisbon's harbor. Today it symbolizes the voyages that made Lisbon powerful, with carved stone representing ropes, Manuel's coat of arms, armillary spheres, and shields with the cross of Manuel's military, called the Order of the Cross.

Cost and Hours: €6, €12 combo-ticket saves you €2 if you also visit the cloister at the Monastery of Jerónimos, free first Sun of every month, May-Sept Tue-Sun 10:00-18:30, off-season until 17:30, closed Mon, last entry 30 minutes before closing, tel. 213-620-034.

Visiting the Tower: This was the last sight sailors saw as they left, and the first as they returned, loaded with gold, spices, and social diseases. When the tower was built, the river went nearly to the walls of the monastery, and the tower was mid-river. Its interior is pretty bare, but the views of the bridge, river, and Cristo Rei statue are worth the 120 steps.

The floatplane on the grassy lawn is a monument to the first flight across the

---

Eating in Belém

You'll find snack bars at Belém Tower, a cafeteria at the Maritime Museum, and fun little restaurants along Rua de Belém, between the National Coach Museum and the monastery. Here are a few other eateries worth checking out:

Restaurante Os Jerónimos is a busy little place good for fresh fish, where hardworking Carlos treats his customers well and serves fine €10 meals (Sun-Fri 12:00-22:30, closed Sat, Rua de Belém 74, tel. 213-638-423, next to renowned Casa Pastéis de Belém pastry café, see page 67).

Pão Pão Queijo Queijo ("Bread Bread Cheese Cheese") serves quick and tasty sandwiches, salads, kebabs, and shawarma sandwiches for less than €5. Place your order at the bar, then eat at tables outside, in the crowded upstairs dining room, or get it to go and picnic in the park across the street (€8 combo plates, Tue-Sat 10:00-24:00, Sun 10:00-20:00, closed Mon, Rua de Belém 124, tel. 213-626-369).

Restaurant Row: Many more fine places with outdoor seating are in the restaurant row behind the McDonald's that faces the park, including **Floresta de Belém,** the local favorite for their home-style Portuguese cooking, such as tasty grilled sardines and *feijoada* bean stew. They have minimal seating inside, but two cozy terraces outside (daily 11:00-23:00 but closed Sept, Praça Afonso de Albuquerque 1A, tel. 213-636-307).

South Atlantic (Portugal to Brazil) in 1922. The original plane (which beat Charles Lindbergh's *Spirit of Saint Louis* across the North Atlantic by five years) is in Belém's Maritime Museum.

If you're choosing between towers, the Monument to the Discoveries is probably the better choice, because it offers a better view of the monastery. Both towers are interesting to see from the outside, whether or not you go up.

Ferry from Belém to Porto Brandão

For a delightfully untouristy little adventure, consider having lunch across the river in **Porto Brandão.** The ferry terminal is immediately in front of the National Coach Museum, across a busy road and train tracks (€1.65 each way, 8-minute cruise, ferries depart on the hour and half hour except hourly from 13:30-15:30, last ferry departs 23:00 weekdays and 22:00 weekends; for a memorable Tejo experience, tall men can use the urinal while sticking their head out the porthole). Boats continue to Trafaria before returning to Belém via Porto Brandão. Upon arrival, carefully confirm return times.

Porto Brandão is a tiny (and dead) three-street town whose harborfront square has several good fish restaurants. I like cozy, blue-and-white-tiled **Restaurante Porto Brandão** (€10-20 fish meals, daily 12:00-15:00 & 18:00-23:00, Rua Bento Jesus Caraça 25, tel. 212-959-145). Their *bacalhau à lagareiro* is for garlic lovers. The *cataplana* (a traditional fish-and-veggie stew) and seafood fondue meals are made for two but stuff three (€15-20/person).

Shopping in Lisbon

Lisbon—Portugal's capital city—has shopping opportunities that run the gamut from flea markets to the country's biggest shopping mall.

Market
The market closest to downtown is Mercado da Ribeira. The recently renovated western section highlights Portuguese gastronomy. Local chefs have adopted famous recipes for sampling, and the casual vibe makes for a fun, on-the-move lunch (produce section Mon-Sat 6:00-14:00, dining section daily 10:00-24:00, Metro: Cais do Sodré).

Flea Markets
On Tuesdays and Saturdays, the Feira da Ladra flea market attracts bargain hunters to Campo de Santa Clara in the Alfama (8:00-15:00, best in morning). A coin market jingles at Mercado da Ribeira, listed above, on Cais do Sodré (Sun 9:00-13:00).

Vasco da Gama Mall
The finest shopping mall in town fills the grand entryway to the 1998 World Expo site at the Oriente train/Metro station. It's well worth a trip out here to feel the pulse of today's Portuguese society, enjoy Parque das Nações, and take in the modern architecture (daily 9:00-24:00).

Centro Colombo Shopping Mall
This is the largest shopping center in Spain or Portugal. More than 400 shops—including FNAC's biggest department store, 10 movie screens, 60 restaurants, and a health club—sit atop what they claim is Europe's biggest underground parking lot and under a vast, entertaining play center. There's plenty to amuse children here, and the place offers a fine look at workaday Lisbon (shops open daily 10:00-22:00, food court and cinemas remain open until 24:00, pick up a map at info desk, Metro: Colégio Militar/Luz takes you right there, tel. 217-113-636).

Armazéns do Chiado
This shopping center's six surprisingly modern floors connect Lisbon's lower and upper towns. It's a stop on "The Bairro Alto and Chiado Stroll" described earlier in this chapter, and has a lively food court on the sixth floor. The FNAC department store hides

behind an old facade and is known for its helpful English-speaking staff. The mall is open daily from 10:00 to 22:00 (eateries about 12:00-23:00, www.armazensdochiado.com).

Here's how to find the mall: If you approach from Chiado, take Rua Garrett, which dead-ends at the main entrance. If coming from the Baixa, head up Rua da Assunção toward the mall, where you'll find three subtle entrances on Rua do Crucifixo—through the Sports Zone store (take their escalators up into the mall), at #113, or at #89 (where small, simple, unmarked doorways lead to elevators).

Lisbon Shop

If you need a souvenir with Lisbon's trademarks—sardines, fado, or trolleys—look no further than this large and inviting store run by the city TI. Music, books, T-shirts, and trinkets are more affordable here than in other shops in the Baixa (daily 9:30-19:30, Rua do Arsenal 13, tel. 210-312-802, www.askmelisboa.com).

A Vida Portuguesa

Located just two blocks from the Armazéns do Chiado shopping center, this is the best shop I found for genuine traditional Portuguese products, from stationery and toiletries to toys and jewelry (Mon-Sat 10:00-20:00, closed Sun, Rua Anchieta 11, tel. 213-465-073, www.avidaportuguesa.com).

El Corte Inglés

The Spanish mega-department store has arrived in Lisbon with a huge store at the top of Edward VII Park, offering an enormous supermarket with great picnic supplies, a food court, a cinema, and much more (Mon-Sat 10:00-22:00, Sun 10:00-20:00, Avenida António Augusto de Aguiar 31, Metro: São Sebastião, near Gulbenkian Museum, tel. 213-711-700).

Entertainment in Lisbon

NIGHTLIFE

Nightlife in the Baixa seems to be little more than loitering prostitutes and litter stirred by the wind. Head instead up to the Bairro Alto for fado halls, bars, and the Miradouro de São Pedro de Alcântara (view terrace), a pleasant place to hang out. Nearby Rua Diario de Noticias is lined with busy bars and fun crowds spilling onto the street.

The Docas

The trendy hot spot for Lisbon's young people is the dock district under the 25th of April Bridge. The Docas (DOH-kash) is a 400-yard-long strip of warehouses turned into pricey restaurants and nightclubs (particularly Doca de Alcântara and Doca de Santo

Amaro). Popular places include Hawaii, Buddha, Havana, and Doca 6 (catch a taxi or trolley #15E from Praça da Figueira to the Avenida Infante Santo stop, take overpass, then a 10-minute walk toward bridge; or bus #714 from Praça da Figueira, ask driver for *"Paragem Docas"*). If you're returning late, night bus #201 starts at 1:00 in the morning and runs every 30 minutes to Cais do Sodré, where you can walk 15 minutes or connect with night bus #205 or #207 to Rossio.

Pink Street

This happening, crazy street (much easier to get to than the Docas) is a short walk downhill from Chiado and a block inland from Praça Duque da Terceira in the Cais do Sodré neighborhood. Rua Nova do Carvalho, otherwise known as "Pink Street," was once notorious as the sailors' red-light zone. Now the prostitutes are just painted onto the walls, and the made-over street is painted a bright pink. After the bars in other neighborhoods close, late-night revelers hike 10 minutes from Chiado down Rua do Alecrim to reach Pink Street. Surrounded by largely uninhabited Pombaline buildings, Pink Street's four bars are allowed to make noise—and they do—until late in the night.

Pensão Amor ("House of Love") is a velvety place for a cocktail. Wallpapered with sexy memories of the days when it was a brothel, it's a grungy tangle of corners to hang out in and enjoy a drink (or just stare at the wallpaper), often against a backdrop of live jazz (no food, Rua Nova do Carvalho 38, also possible to enter from top at Rua do Alecrim 19, tel. 213-143-399).

Sol e Pesca Bar, a nostalgic reminder of the sailor-and-fisherman heritage of this street, sells drinks and preserved food in tins. Just browse the shelves of classic €1-6 tinned seafood—from pâté and sardines to caviar (€1 extra to eat from a tin at a table)—and wash down your salty seafood tapas with a glass of wine amid the lures and nets (Rua Nova do Carvalho 44, tel. 213-467-203).

Bar de Velha Senhora ("The Old Lady") is a dark bar with live music most nights starting at 23:00 on its cozy little stage (burlesque Thu-Sat, jazz and other music on other nights, no cover, Rua Nova do Carvalho 38, tel. 213-468-479).

Povo Lisboa is a trendy little bar serving delightful Portuguese tapas (from 18:00) and enlivening things with fado later on (Sun and Tue-Thu 21:30, no cover, just buy a drink, light food, Rua Nova do Carvalho 32, tel. 213-473-403).

Evening Stroll

While not as big a deal as in Spain, the people of Lisbon enjoy an early evening stroll after work and before dinner when the weather is balmy. When it comes to weather, Lisboners are pretty spoiled. If it's even a little blustery, they'll likely stay in. But when it's nice, in the summer, you'll find lots of people out strolling. Four good plac-es: Rua Augusta through the heart of the Baixa district; along the seaside promenade near the Belém Tower; along the fine riverfront promenade at Parque das Nações; and the river walk at Ribeira das Naus (from the water at Praça do Comércio to Cais do Sodré).

▲▲FADO

Fado is the folk music of Lisbon's back streets. Since the mid-1800s, it's been the Lisbon blues—mournfully beautiful and haunting ballads about lost sailors, broken hearts, and bittersweet romance. While generally sad, fado can also be jaunty—in a nostalgic way—and captivating. A stout 60-year-old widow singing fado can be invitingly sexy.

Fado has become one of Lisbon's favorite late-night tourist traps, but it's easy to find a convivial and rustic bar without the high prices and tour groups. Both the Bairro Alto and the Alfama have small, informal fado restaurants. Go either for a late dinner (after 21:00) or an even later evening of drinks and music. Homemade "fado tonight" *(fado esta noite)* signs in Portuguese are good news, but even a restaurant filled with tourists can come with good food and fine fado. I like "fado vadio," a kind of open-mic fado evening when amateurs line up at the door of neighborhood dives for their chance to warble.

Prices for a fado performance vary greatly. Many have a steep cover charge, while others just expect you to buy a meal. Appetiz-ers, bread, or cheese that appear on your table aren't free—if you nibble, you'll pay. Send them back if you don't want to be charged. Assume any place recommended by a hotel is a tourist trap with prices bloated by €15 kickbacks (don't even let the hotel call to con-firm your reservation—or they'll take that kickback). Both elegant, high-end places and holes-in-the-wall generally let non-diners in late for the cost of a drink or a small cover charge.

Fado in the Bairro Alto

In the Bairro Alto, wander around Rua Diario de Noticias and neighboring streets. **Canto do Camões,** run by friendly, English-speaking Gabriel, is easy to reserve and has good music and tasty food. Call ahead to assure a seat (open at 20:00, music from 20:30 until after midnight; €27 meal required—includes appetizer, 3 courses, water, and wine; after 22:00 €12 minimum for two drinks; from Rua da Misericordia, go 2 blocks uphill on Travessa da Es-pera to #38; tel. 213-465-464). When it's busy, the room feels like a stage show, with 25 or 30 tables filled mostly with tourists, all enjoying classic fado. Relax, spend some time, and close your eyes, or make eye contact with the singer. Let the music and wine col-laborate.

Fado

Fado songs reflect Portugal's bittersweet relationship with the sea. Fado means "fate"—how fate deals with Portugal's adventurers...and the women they leave behind.

These are songs of both sadness and hope, a bittersweet emotion called *saudade* (meaning yearning or nostalgia). The lyrics reflect the pining for a loved one across the water, hopes for a future reunion, remembrances of a rosy past or dreams of a better future, and the yearning for what might have been if fate had not intervened. (Fado can also be bright and happy when the song is about the virtues of cities such as Lisbon or Coimbra, or of the warmth of a typical *casa portuguesa*.)

The songs are often in a minor key. The singer *(fadista)* is accompanied by a 12-string Portuguese *guitarra* (with a round body like a mandolin) or other stringed instruments unique to Portugal. Many singers crescendo into the first word of the verse, like a moan emerging from deep inside. Though the songs are often sad, the singers rarely overact—they plant themselves firmly and sing stoically in the face of fate.

A verse from a typical fado song goes:

> *O waves of the salty sea,*
> *where do you get your salt?*
> *From the tears shed by the women in black*
> *on the beaches of Portugal.*

Restaurante Adega do Ribatejo is a homey place crowded with locals and tourists nightly (except Sun) from around 20:30 to 24:00. Just around the corner from Canto do Camões and less touristy (almost anti-touristy), you can sit down here and just pay for whatever you want to eat or drink with no required minimum (€15 meals, Mon-Sat from 19:00, closed Sun, Rua Diario de Noticias 23, tel. 213-468-343). After 22:30 you're welcome to just buy a drink and enjoy the music for free.

Fado in Chiado, a sterile 50-minute performance in a small modern theater, is for tourists who don't want to stay out late or mess with a restaurant. Sitting with other tourists and without food or drink, you'll enjoy four musicians: a man and a woman singing, a guitarist, and a man on the Portuguese guitar, which gives fado its balalaika charm (€17, daily at 19:00 except Sun, conveniently located in Chiado at Rua da Misericordia 14, on second floor of in Cine Theatro Gymnasio, tel. 961-717-778).

Fado in the Alfama

While often pretty lonely and dead after dark, the Alfama has several bars offering fado with their meals—just head uphill from the Fado Museum. Some bars are geared for tourists and tour groups, but others feel organic, spontaneous, and part of the neighborhood culture. While schedules at any particular place can be inconsistent, if you hike up Rua São Pedro de Alcântara to the Church of São Miguel, you'll hear the music wafting out from hole-in-the-wall eateries and be greeted by men hustling business for their fado restaurants. Generally, you simply pay for the meal and enjoy the music as included entertainment. If it's late and there's room, you can just buy a drink.

A Baiuca, a tiny fun-loving restaurant, offers my favorite Alfama fado experience. A Baiuca—the name means a very rough tavern—packs people in and serves up spirited "fado vadio" (open mic for amateurs) with traditional home-cooking and lots of wine. As the English-speaking manager, Isabel, likes to say, "Fado needs wine." This intimate place is a neighborhood affair and has surround sound—as everyone seems to get into the music (€25 minimum, unless you come very late when you can just buy a drink, best singing Thu-Mon 20:00-24:00; reservations smart, in the heart of the Alfama, just off Rua São Pedro up the hill from Fado Museum, at Rua de São Miguel 20, tel. 218-867-284). When the door is closed, they're full, but you can peek at the action through the window around to the left.

Clube de Fado is much classier—one of the best places in town to hear quality fado. While a bit pricey, there's not a bad seat in the house. Music plays nightly in this formal yet intimate setting. When busy, the musicians switch between two adjacent halls, giving waiters time to serve between sets, and diners get music about half the time (plan on €50 for dinner with wine, plus a €7.50 cover charge, meals from 20:00, dinner reservations required, music 21:30 until after midnight; after 23:00, pay just a €10 cover charge plus cost of your drink; around corner from cathedral at Rua São João da Praça 94, tel. 218-852-704).

Casa de Linhares, a block downhill from Clube de Fado, offers similar quality fado and an even nicer space, with dinner served under the stone vaults of a 16th-century palace (plan about €40 for dinner, €15 cover for music, nightly from 20:00, after 22:00 €15 with drink purchase, Beco dos Armazéns Do Linho 2, tel. 218-865-088).

BULLFIGHTS, SOCCER, CONCERTS, AND MOVIES

Tickets to all bullfights, soccer games, concerts, and other events are sold at the green **ABEP kiosk** at the southern end of Praça dos Restauradores (daily 9:00-20:00, also sells city transit pass and LisboaCard, across the street from TI).

▲▲▲Portuguese Bullfight

If you always felt sorry for the bull, this is Toro's Revenge: In a Portuguese bullfight, the matador is brutalized along with the bull. Lisbon hosts only about a dozen fights a year, but if you're in town for one, it's an unforgettable experience.

In Act I, the horseman *(cavaleiro)* skillfully plants four beribboned barbs in the bull's back while trying to avoid the

leather-padded horns. The horses are the short, stocky Lusitano breed, with excellent balance. In Act II, a colorfully clad eight-man suicide squad (called *forçados*) enters the ring and lines up single file facing the bull. With testosterone sloshing everywhere, the leader taunts the bull—slapping his knees and yelling, *"touro!"*—then braces himself for a collision that can be heard all the way up in the cheap seats. As he hangs onto the bull's head, his buddies pile on, trying to wrestle the bull to a standstill. Finally, one guy hangs on to *o touro's* tail and "water-skis" behind him. (In Act III, the *ambulância* arrives.)

Unlike the Spanish *corrida de toros*, the bull is not killed in front of the crowd at the Portuguese *tourada*...but it is killed later. (Some brave bulls with only superficial wounds are spared to fight another day.) Spanish aficionados insist that Portuguese fights are actually crueler, since they humiliate the bull, rather than fight him as a fellow warrior. Animal-rights groups enliven the scene before each fight.

The ring is small, so there are no bad seats. To sit nearly at ringside, try the cheapest *bancada* seats, on the generally half-empty and unmonitored main floor (Metro: Campo Pequeno). The ring is a spectacular, Moorish-domed brick structure that bears a resemblance to Madrid's bullring. After five years of remodeling, it reopened with a shopping mall underneath and a retractable roof overhead for concerts. It hosts a variety of restaurants inside, oddly including an Argentine steak restaurant. Maybe the beef served was in the ring earlier?

Fights are generally held on Thursday at 20:00 and on Sunday afternoons from Easter through September. Important note: Half the fights are simply Spanish-type *corridas* without the killing. For the real slam-bam Portuguese-style fight, confirm that there will be *grupo de forçados* ("bull grabbers"). Tickets are always available at the door (€20-50, no surcharge, tel. 217-932-143 to confirm; tickets sold at the ABEP kiosk on Praça dos Restauradores add a 10 percent surcharge).

Soccer

Lisbon is home to two *futebol* teams, Benfica and Sporting CP, which means there are lots of games (1-2/week Aug-May, tickets €20 and up) and lots of team spirit. Benfica, with the red jerseys, plays at the 65,400-seat Stadium of Light near the Centro Colombo mall (Estádio da Luz; Metro: Colegio Militar/Luz, www.slbenfica.pt). Sporting CP, with the green-and-white jerseys, plays at the 50,000-seat Estádio José Alvalade to the north of Lisbon's center (Metro: Campo Grande, www.sporting.pt). Tickets are generally available at the stadium or at the ABEP kiosk on Praça dos Restauradores.

Concerts

You can hear classical music by national and city orchestras at the Gulbenkian Museum and at the cultural center in Belém (www.ccb.pt). Traditional Portuguese theater plays in the National Theater on Rossio and in theaters along Rua das Portas de Santo Antão (the "eating lane") stretching north from Rossio. For popular music, these days you're more likely to find rock, jazz, Brazilian, and African music than traditional fado. The monthly *Agenda Cultural* provides the most up-to-date listing of world music, arts, and entertainment (free at TI, €0.50 at newsstands, online at www.agendalx.pt, in Portuguese only).

Movies

In Lisbon, unlike in Spain, most films are shown in the original language with subtitles. (That's one reason the Portuguese speak better English than the Spanish.) Many of Lisbon's theaters are classy, complete with assigned seats, ushers, and intermissions. Check the newspaper to see what's playing, or drop by the ABEP kiosk at Praça dos Restauradores, where a list of all the movies playing in town is taped to a side window (on the left). São Jorge Theater, located midway up Avenida da Liberdade, is a grand old Art Deco movie palace showing festival treats; it's run by the same cultural organization in charge of the São Jorge Castle and the Monument to the Discoveries. More modern options are in malls like Colombo, El Corte Inglés, or at the Monumental complex in the ritzy Saldanha neighborhood (Metro: Saldanha).

Sleeping in Lisbon

With a few exceptions, cheaper hotels downtown feel tired and well-worn. Singles cost nearly the same as doubles. If you're on a tight budget and want to stay in the center, consider Lisbon's famously classy hostels, which welcome travelers of all ages. Addresses such as 26-3 stand for building #26, third floor (which is the fourth floor in American terms).

Be sure to book in advance if you'll be in Lisbon during its festival—Festas de Lisboa—the last three weeks of June, when parades, street parties, concerts, and fireworks draw crowds to the city. Conventions can clog Lisbon at any time.

IN THE CENTER

Central as can be, the Baixa district bustles with lots of shops, traffic, people, street musicians, pedestrian areas, and urban intensity.

On Rossio

$$$ Internacional Design Hotel has 55 hip, ultra-modern double rooms centrally located at the southeast corner of Rossio. Each of its four floors has a different theme—pop, Zen, tribal, and urban. Having coffee in their expansive breakfast room overlooking Rossio is a fantastic way to start the day. I've listed its expensive rack rates, but you can often get a room for a 10 to 20 percent discount by booking ahead online (Db-€120-400 depending on size, Db with pull-out child's bed-€500, buffet breakfast in bright room overlooking Rossio, air-con, elevator, Wi-Fi, underground parking nearby-€15/day, Rua da Betesga 3, tel. 213-240-990, www.idesignhotel.com, book@idesignhotel.com).

$$$ Hotel Métropole keeps its elegant 1920s style throughout 36 carefully appointed but slightly worn rooms. It's overpriced, but you're paying for the prime location. The quieter back rooms are smaller, but cost the same unless you ask for a break. Prices drop by a third in slow times. Don't be shy; ask for a 10 percent Rick Steves discount when you reserve (Sb-€110-200, Db-€130-200, extra bed-€50, check website for discounts, buffet breakfast, air-con, elevator, free Wi-Fi in lobby, Rossio 30, tel. 213-219-030, www.metropole-lisbon.com, metropole@themahotels.com).

On Praça dos Restauradores

$$$ Hotel Avenida Palace, the most characteristic five-star splurge in town, was built with Rossio Station in 1892 to greet big-shot travelers. Back then, trains were new, and Rossio was the only station in town. The lounges are sumptuous, dripping with chandeliers, and the 82 rooms mix elegance with 21st-century comforts

---

Sleep Code

Abbreviations   **(€1 = about $1.40, country code: 351)**
S = Single, **D** = Double/Twin, **T** = Triple, **Q** = Quad, **b** = bathroom, **s** = shower only.

Price Rankings
  $$$ Higher Priced—Most rooms €115 or more.
    $$ Moderately Priced—Most rooms between €65-115.
      $ Lower Priced—Most rooms €65 or less.

Unless otherwise noted, credit cards are accepted, tax is included in the price, English is spoken, breakfast is included, and Wi-Fi is generally free. Prices can change without notice; verify the hotel's current rates online or by email. For the best prices, always book directly with the hotel.

(Sb-€194, Db-€228, more expensive suites available, reserve on website for substantial discounts, air-con, elevator, Wi-Fi, laundry service, free parking, hotel's sign is on Praça dos Restauradores but entrance is at Rua 1 de Dezembro 123, down a small alleyway next to Starbucks, tel. 213-218-121, www.hotelavenidapalace.pt, reservas@hotelavenidapalace.pt).

$$$ VIP Executive Suites Eden rents 134 slick and contemporary compact apartments (with small kitchens). It has a rooftop

swimming pool and breakfast terrace with commanding city, castle, and river views. The building used to be a 1930s cinema, hence the Art Deco architecture and the slightly pie-shaped rooms. Perfectly located at the Rossio end of Avenida da Liberdade, this is a clean, quiet pool of modernity amid the ramshackle charm of Lisbon. It's also an intriguing option for groups or families of four (Db studio-€95-129, 2-bedroom apartment with bed-and-sofa combo that can sleep 4 people-€139-189, breakfast-€9, check website for deals, air-con, elevator, Praça dos Restauradores 24, tel. 213-216-600, www.viphotels.com, res.eden@viphotels.com).

Near Praça da Figueira

$$$ Hotel Lisboa Tejo (leezh-BOH-ah TAY-zhoo) is an oasis of 58 comfy ocean-blue rooms with hardwood floors (Sb-€60-113, Db-€70-131, 10 percent discount with this book only when reserved direct through hotel, crowded breakfast buffet, air-con, elevator, Wi-Fi; from southeast corner of Praça da Figueira, walk one block down Rua dos Condes de Monsanto and turn left to

LISBON

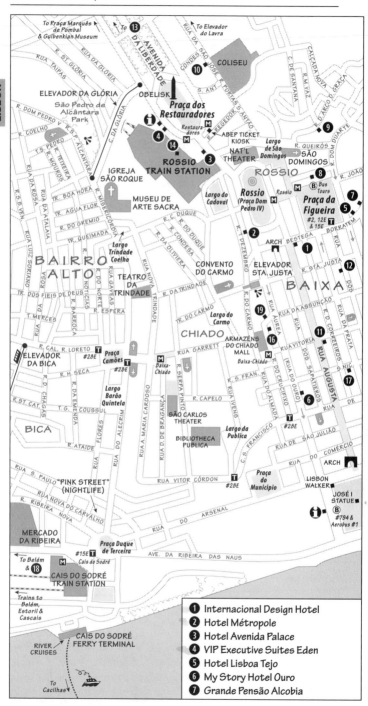

To Praça Marquês de Pombal & Gulbenkian Museum

To 13

To Elevador do Lavra

RUA DAS PORTAS DE SÃO ANTÃO

RUA DE SÃO JOSÉ
CONDES DE SÃO JOSÉ

COLISEU

10

CALÇADA NOVA
C. DE SANTANA
R.M. VAZ

AVENIDA DA LIBERDADE

RUA DA GLÓRIA

RUA ST. GLÓRIA

RUA TAIPAS

R. DOM PEDRO V

R. SÃO PEDRO

R. COELHO

R. MEDROS

R. TEIXEIRA

R.D. B. VEN.

R. LUIZ SORIANO

ELEVADOR DA GLÓRIA

São Pedro de Alcântara Park

OBELISK

Praça dos Restauradores

Restauradores

M

ABEP TICKET KIOSK

NAT'L THEATER

4

14

M

3

Largo de São Domingos

SÃO DOMINGOS

8

ROSSIO

R. QUEIRÓS

R. DOM DUARTE

R. ARCO D. GRAÇA

9

R. JOÃO

B Bus Tours

M

Rossio

7

5

Praça da Figueira

#2, 12E & 15E

T

IGREJA SÃO ROQUE

MUSEU DE ARTE SACRA

ROSSIO TRAIN STATION

Largo do Cadoval

Rossio (Praça Dom Pedro IV)

BORKATEM

R. DOM PEDRO V

TR. BOA HORA

R. AGUA FLOR

R. DO GRÉMIO

TR. QUEIMADA

Largo Trindade Coelho

R.C. DUQUE

R. DO DUQUE

R. DA OLIVEIRA

R. CONDESA

R. T. DEZEMBRO

2

ARCH BESTEGA

1

ELEVADOR STA. JUSTA

R. STA. JUSTA

12

BAIRRO ALTO

R. DA ATALAIA

R. DO NORTE

R. DAS GAVEAS

RUA NOVA TRINDADE

R. DA TRINDADE

CONVENTO DO CARMO

R. DO CARMO

R. DO OURO

BAIXA

TEATRO DA TRINDADE

TR. DOS FIÉIS DE DEUS

R. NOTICIAS

R. BARROCA

R. ESPERA

TR. DO CARMO

Largo do Carmo

19

RUA DA ASSUNÇÃO

RUA AUREA

RUA DA PRATA

T. MERCES

CHIADO

RUA GARRETT

16

ARMAZÉNS DO CHIADO MALL

RUA VITORIA

11

RUA DOS CORREEIROS

RUA AUGUSTA

ELEVADOR DA BICA

R. CAL. R. LORETO

Praça Camões

#28E

T

Baixa-Chiado

M

Baixa-Chiado

RUA DO CARMO

17

R.D.

R. H. SECA

R.D. A. MEDA

COUSSUL

Largo Barão Quintela

SERPA PINTO

R.S. FRAN.

R. DO CRUCIFIXO

R. DA PRATA

R.C. D.S.

6

R.S. NIC.

R.D. A. MEDA

#28E

R. ST. CAT.

T.G. MATA

BICA

R. ATAIDE

RUA D. DE BRAGANÇA

SÃO CARLOS THEATER

R. CAPELO

Largo da Publica

RUA DE SÃO JULIÃO

RUA DO COMÉRCIO

T

#28E

RUA DE S. FRANCISCO

RUA S. PAULO "PINK STREET" (NIGHTLIFE)

RUA NOVA DO CARVALHO

R. RIBEIRA NOVA

MERCADO DA RIBEIRA

BIBLIOTHECA PUBLICA

RUA MARIA CARDOSO

RUA D. DO ALECRIM

RUA VITOR CÓRDON

T

#28E

Praça do Município

ARCH

LISBON WALKER

JOSÉ I STATUE

RUA DO ARSENAL

RUA

AVE. DA RIBEIRA DAS NAUS

i

#794 & Aerobus #1

To Belém & 18

Praça Duque de Terceira

#15E T

Cais do Sodré

M

CAIS DO SODRÉ TRAIN STATION

Trains to Belém, Estoril & Cascais

RIVER CRUISES

CAIS DO SODRÉ FERRY TERMINAL

To Cacilhas

1 Internacional Design Hotel
2 Hotel Métropole
3 Hotel Avenida Palace
4 VIP Executive Suites Eden
5 Hotel Lisboa Tejo
6 My Story Hotel Ouro
7 Grande Pensão Alcobia

Lisbon Center Hotels

LISBON

8 Pensão Praça da Figueira
9 Pensão Residencial Gerês
10 Residencial Florescente
11 Hotel Duas Nações
12 Norte Guest House
13 To Avenida da Liberdade Area Hotels & Ibis Hotels
14 Lisbon Destination Hostel
15 Home Lisbon Hostel
16 Living Lounge Hostel
17 Lisbon Lounge Hostel
18 To Hotel As Janelas Verdes
19 Laundry

Condes de Monsanto 2; tel. 218-866-182, www.lisboatejohotel. com, reservas@lisboatejohotel.com).

$$ My Story Hotel Ouro has 51 rooms decorated in gold tones—*ouro* in Portuguese. Outside-facing rooms have interesting views, but ask for an inside room for a quiet night's sleep (Sb-€90, Db-€100-110, substantially less off-season, air-con, elevator, Wi-Fi, Rua Áurea 100, tel. 213-400-340, www.mystoryhotels.com, ouro@mystoryhotels.com).

$$ Grande Pensão Alcobia has 42 simple, worn rooms but offers an alternative to higher-priced hotels located in the same part of town. Some upper-floor rooms have views of São Jorge Castle (Sb-€45-60, Db-€50-80, Tb-€90-105, 10 percent discount with this book when reserved direct through hotel, air-con, small elevator, guest computer and Wi-Fi, Poço do Borratem 15, tel. 218-844-150, www.pensaoalcobia.com, reservasalcobia@sapo.pt).

$ Pensão Praça da Figueira is a backpacker place on a quiet back street with youth-hostel prices, a kitchen on every floor, and 37 clean, basic rooms (D-€35-45, Ds-€45-53, Db-€53-63, singles-€7 less, extra bed-€20, breakfast included, 2 flights up with no elevator, Wi-Fi, entrance is at Travessa Nova de São Domingos 9, behind Praça da Figueira, tel. 213-426-757, www.pensaopracadafigueira. com, pensaofigueira@clix.pt).

Near Rossio

$$ Pensão Residencial Gerês rents 20 bright, basic, cozy rooms with older plumbing but without the dingy smokiness that pervades Lisbon's cheaper hotels. Double-paned windows keep out much of the street noise (S-€45, Sb-€55, Db-€60, Tb-€85-100, 10 percent discount only Nov-March with cash and this book, no breakfast, pay Wi-Fi, uphill a block off northeast corner of Rossio, Calçada do Garcia 6, tel. 218-810-497, www.pensaogeres.net, info@pensaogeres.net). The super-sweet Nogueira family speaks some English.

$ Residencial Florescente rents 68 rooms on the "eating lane," a thriving pedestrian street a block off Praça dos Restauradores (Sb-€45-50, Db-€75, bigger twin Db-€75-85, Tb-€85-95, higher prices apply July-Sept, air-con, Wi-Fi, Rua das Portas de Santo Antão 99, tel. 213-426-609, www.residencialflorescente. com, geral@residencialflorescente.com).

$ Hotel Duas Nações offers 73 small, modern rooms in a great location (Db-€65, air-con, pay Wi-Fi, staff can be indifferent, Rua Augusta and Rua da Victoria 41, tel. 213-460-710, www. duasnacoes.com, reservas@duasnacoes.com).

$ Norte Guest House rents 34 small, linoleum-floored rooms. Although a bit dark, it beats a youth hostel—barely (Ds-€29-32, Db-€39-44, Tb/Qb-€44-49, higher prices apply July-Sept, no breakfast, a bit smoky, Wi-Fi, Rua dos Douradores 161, tel. 218-878-941, www.norteguesthouse.com, info@norteguesthouse.com).

Along Avenida da Liberdade

These listings are a 10-minute walk or short Metro ride from the center.

Near Metro: Avenida

$$$ Hotel Lisboa Plaza, a large, plush four-star gem, mixes traditional style with bright-pastel classiness. With 112 rooms, it offers snappy and polite service, all the amenities, and a free glass of port when you check in (Sb-€120-190, Db-€130-200, extra bed-€47, higher prices apply March-June and Sept-Oct, larger "superior" rooms cost 25 percent more, buffet breakfast-€14, air-con, one allergen-free floor, Wi-Fi, parking-€10/day; well-located on a quiet street off busy Avenida da Liberdade, a block from Metro: Avenida, Travessa do Salitre 7; tel. 213-218-218, www.heritage.pt, plaza@heritage.pt). Hotel Lisboa Plaza and its sister, Hotel Britania (listed later), offer a deal in July and August: free entrance to Lisbon's museums for guests who stay at least three nights.

$$ Hotel Botânico, in a blocky, modern building on a characteristic street a steep five-minute walk above Avenida da Liberdade, is quiet—unless there's a demonstration at the Planned Parenthood clinic across the street. The hotel rents 30 modern, business-class rooms; street-side rooms on the top floor have a view of São Jorge Castle (Sb-€45-90, Db-€50-95, Tb-€60-95, air-con, elevator, Wi-Fi, parking, Rua Mãe d'Água 16, tel. 213-420-392, www.hotelbotanico.pt, hotelbotanico@netcabo.pt).

$$ Residêncial Roma, a stark little place, rents 40 simple rooms. It's tucked away on a side street, 50 yards off the big Avenida da Liberdade (Sb-€35-50, Db-€45-70, extra bed-€10-15, air-con, no elevator, Travessa da Glória 22, tel. 213-460-558, www.residenciaroma.com, res.roma@cyclopnet.pt). They also rent apartments (Db-€75-120, €10/extra person).

$$ Hotel Alegria, a fine old establishment with 35 rooms, faces a quiet, inviting park in a peaceful neighborhood 200 yards from the Avenida Metro station. Varnished like a ship, it has sloping hardwood floors and solid furniture (Db-€60-85, third person-€15 extra, breakfast-€6, air-con, elevator, Praça da Alegria 12, tel. 213-220-670, www.alegrianet.com, mail@alegrianet.com).

Others near Avenida da Liberdade

$$$ Hotel Britania maintains its 1940s Art Deco charm throughout its 33 spacious rooms, offering a clean and professional haven on a tranquil street one block off Avenida da Liberdade. Three top-floor suites are decorated in a luxurious Mod Deco style. Run by the Hotel Lisboa Plaza folks (listed earlier), it offers the same four-star standards for the same prices (air-con, elevator, laundry service, Wi-Fi, free street parking or €15/day in next-door garage; from Metro: Avenida stop, walk uphill on boulevard, turn right on Rua Manuel de Jesus Coelho and take first left to Rua Rodrigues Sampaio 17; tel. 213-155-016, www.heritage.pt, britania.hotel@ heritage.pt).

$ Lisbon Dreams Guesthouse has 18 fresh, relaxing, Ikea-like rooms, occupying three apartments and sharing seven bathrooms (S-€50, D-€60, T-€80, discounts often available on website, Wi-Fi and free loaner laptops, laundry service-€6, two shared terraces, kitchen for guest use; Metro: Marquês de Pombal, then take Rua Alexandre Herculano uphill and turn left on Rua Rodrigo da Fonesca, or Metro: Rato, take Rua Alexandre Herculano downhill, then right to reach Rua Rodrigo da Fonesca 29, tel. 213-872-393, www.lisbondreams.com, info@lisbondreams.com).

$ Lisbon Centre Hostel has 31 dorm rooms and some private rooms in a 19th-century building (bed in 3- to 6-bed dorm-€18, D-€68, includes sheets, 24-hour access, elevator, Wi-Fi, café and bar, laundry, luggage storage, Rua Andrade Corvo 46 near Avenida da Liberdade, Metro: Picoas, tel. 213-532-696, www.hihostels. com, lisboa@movijovem.pt).

Boutique Hostels in the Baixa

Among hostel aficionados, Lisbon is famous for having the best hostels anywhere. They welcome travelers of any age and come with an artistic flair and plenty of double rooms. Here are four that are conveniently located in the center of town.

$ Lisbon Destination Hostel feels designed for backpackers—young and old—who appreciate style, peace, and quiet. Located upstairs in the Rossio train station, it provides a wonderful value and experience (85 beds, 23 rooms, €20/bed in 4-10-bed dorms, S-€35, D-€60, Db-€70, Wi-Fi, lockers, movie night in lounge, tel. 213-466-457, www.destinationhostels.com, lisbon@ destinationhostels.com).

$ Home Lisbon Hostel is a little more rough and homey, with free laundry, movies, and friendly management (91 beds, €15/bed in 4- to 8-bed dorms, Rua de São Nicolau 13-2, near corner of Rua dos Fanqueiros, Metro: Baixa-Chiado, tel. 218-885-312, www. mylisbonhome.com, info@mylisbonhome.com).

$ Living Lounge Hostel is clean, modern, and in a very central location near the Baixa-Chiado Metro stop. Each room is uniquely decorated (€18-24/bed in 4- to 8-bed mixed dorms, S-€30-37, D-€26-32; includes sheets and towels; air-con, elevator, lockers, laundry service, bike rentals, free tours and excursions, free guest computer and Wi-Fi, Rua Crucifixo 116, second floor, tel. 213-

461-078, www.livingloungehostel.com, info@livingloungehostel. com).

$ Lisbon Lounge Hostel, run by the same folks as the Living Lounge Hostel above, offers the same amenities, style and prices, but no singles. It's in the Baixa, roughly midway between Praça da Figueira and Praça do Comércio (€18-24/bed in 4- to 8-bed mixed dorms, D-€24-32, Rua de São Nicolau 41, tel. 213-462-061, www. lisbonloungehostel.com, info@lisbonloungehostel.com).

AWAY FROM THE CENTER

$$$ Hotel As Janelas Verdes, next door to the Museum of Ancient Art, is another of Hotel Lisboa Plaza's sister properties. An 18th-century mansion that's now a boutique hotel, it has 29 cushy rooms and comfortably elegant public spaces. The third-floor library overlooks the river (Sb/Db-€160-300, check website for specials, air-con, elevator, Wi-Fi, Rua das Janeles Verdes 7, bus #714 stops nearby, tel. 213-968-143, www.heritage.pt, janelas.verdes@ heritage.pt).

$$ *Ibis Hotels:* Ibis hotels offer no-stress, no-character rooms for a good price in soulless areas away from the center—but near handy Metro stations. Each has air-conditioning and €5 breakfasts. One child under 12 stays for free and a third adult is €10 (www. ibishotel.com). **Ibis Liberdade** has the best location (70 rooms, Sb/ Db-€80, 2 blocks uphill from Avenida da Liberdade's Hotel Tivoli, Metro: Avenida, Rua Barata Salgueiro 53, tel. 213-300-630), followed by **Ibis Saldanha** (116 rooms, Sb/Db-€70, 2-minute walk from Metro: Saldanha, Avenida Casal Ribeiro 23, tel. 213-191-690).

APARTMENTS

Cross-Pollinate is an online booking agency representing B&Bs and apartments in a handful of European cities, including Lisbon. Unlike huge aggregator websites like HomeAway or VRBO, Cross-Pollinate handpicks its listings. Search their website for a listing you like, then submit your reservation online. If the place is available, you'll be charged a small deposit and emailed the location and check-in details. Policies vary from owner to owner, but in most cases you'll pay the balance on arrival in cash. Lisbon listings range from a Rossio guesthouse room for two for €70 per night to a two-bedroom Alfama apartment sleeping four for €100 per night. Minimum stays vary from one to three nights (US tel. 800-270-1190, www.cross-pollinate.com, info@cross-pollinate.com).

Eating in Lisbon

Each district of the city comes with fun and characteristic restaurants. Ideally, have one dinner with a fado performance—several good options for music with your meal are listed in this section, with more fado options described earlier, under "Entertainment in Lisbon."

Food Tours in Lisbon: To simultaneously eat good food, learn about Portuguese cuisine, and meet a knowledgeable local guide, consider taking one of the food tours offered by Inside Lisbon, Eat Portugal, or Eat Drink Walk. Their tours are a good value—informative and tasty—filling you in while filling you up.

SNACK BARS

Lisbon seems enthusiastic about serving quick, light meals at characteristic bars. On just about any street, you can belly up to a bar, observe, and order what looks good for a tasty, memorable, and extremely cheap meal. You'll see lots of *pastel de bacalhau* (€1), Lisbon's ubiquitous and delicious cod cake. Strangely, this national dish of Portugal comes from Norway—salted cod. It's never fresh, always salty. Another good standby is a *bifana*, a pork sandwich made with a secret sauce to give it character.

Below the Castle and Above the Alfama

Farol de Santa Luzia, which offers a nice seafood feast with a delicate and delightful dining area, is a favorite of mine for lunch or dinner at the top of the Alfama. A family-run place with a local clientele, they offer the Algarve *cataplana* style of cooking (€7-8 daily specials; €26 big *cataplana* of meat, fish, or shellfish for two; indoor seating only, Mon-Sat 12:00-15:00 & 18:30-23:00, closed Sun, Largo Santa Luzia 5, across from Santa Luzia viewpoint terrace, tiny sign, tel. 218-863-884, Andre and family).

Lunch on Largo do Contador Mor: Two basic restaurants—**A Tasquinha Restaurante** and **Comidas de Santiago**—feed hungry tourists on this leafy square just below the castle. Both specialize in plates of grilled sardines *(sardinhas grelhadas)* and are handy for a simple lunch.

Near Largo Rodrigues de Freitas: For more of an adventure with your meal, walk past Largo das Portas do Sol and follow the trolley tracks along Rua de São Tomé to a square called Largo Rodrigues de Freitas—if riding trolley #12E, it's the first stop over the big hill. **Restaurante Frei Papinhas** is a classic, family-run, hole-in-the-wall where you can feast on fresh seafood for €10 a plate with the neighborhood crowd. Dine inside or on rickety tables across the street in a charming square, where you can watch the trolleys rattle by (daily, Rua de São Tome 13, tel. 218-866-471).

Appetizers Aren't Free

In Portugal, there's no such thing as a free munch. Appetizers brought to your table before you order (such as olives, bread, and fancy pâtés) are not free. So if you don't want to pay for them, just push them aside or wave them away when the waiter brings them. Don't eat any of it—not even one olive—or you'll be charged (only €1-2 for the simpler appetizers, but it's disturbing if you don't expect it).

RESTAURANTS DEEP IN THE ALFAMA

While the Bairro Alto is far livelier at night and has a better energy, the Alfama still has a unique charm. My favorite places for dinner with fado (the funky, characteristic **A Baiuca** and the more formal and classy **Clube de Fado**) are described earlier under "Entertainment in Lisbon."

Restaurante Santo Antonio de Alfama, buried scenically in the Alfama, is bohemian yet dressy and intimate (notice the classic cinema theme) and serves a global cuisine with creative €9 tapas and €15-20 main courses. While it's tempting to cobble together a tapas meal, I liked the main dishes better. On a balmy evening, the small courtyard seating overlooking the classic Alfama square offers a romantic setting (Wed-Sun 12:30-16:30 & 19:30-24:00, Beco de São Miguel 7, tel. 218-881-328).

BAIRRO ALTO, LISBON'S "HIGH TOWN"

The Bairro Alto is hopping lately with plenty of energy and fun eateries opening up all the time. For a characteristic meal in Old World surroundings, it's hard to beat. When considering the Bairro Alto listings, remember that the Chiado listings (which follow) are just a few minutes' walk away.

Fado with Dinner in Bairro Alto: For a most memorable dining experience with live fado music in the Bairro Alto, consider **Canto do Camões** (more formal and subdued, Travessa da Espera 38) or **Restaurante Adega do Ribatejo** (more rough and casual, Rua Diario de Noticias 23).

Restaurante Bota Alta ("The Old Boot") is a classic—if a bit touristy—little eatery with a timeless Portuguese ambience, tight seating, and reliably good food. Portions are big, reservations are smart, and Paulo offers a fun dessert sampler plate (€10-15 main dishes, Mon-Sat 12:00-14:30, 19:00-23:00, closed Sun, straight up from lottery kiosk in front of São Roque Church, at corner of Travessa da Queimada and Rua da Atalaia, tel. 213-427-959).

A Primavera do Jerónimo is a quintessential Bairro Alto joint

To Praça Marquês de Pombal & Gulbenkian Museum
To 26
RUA DE SÃO JOSÉ
To Elevador do Lavra & 25
COLISEU
AVENIDA DA LIBERDADE
CONDES DE SÃO JOSÉ
R. ST. GLÓRIA
RUA DA GLÓRIA
RUA TAIPAS
OBELISK
23
24
R. ANT. P. PORTAS DE SANTO ANTÃO
R. C. DE SANTANA
R. M. VAZ
CALÇADA DO GRAÇA
R. D. ARCO D. GRAÇA

13 ELEVADOR DA GLÓRIA
São Pedro de Alcântara Park
R. DOM PEDRO
R. COELHO
14
12
R.S. PEDRO
T. S. PEDRO
R. MOUROS
TEIXEIRA
Praça dos Restauradores
Restaura-dores
ABEP TICKET KIOSK
NAT'L THEATER
Largo de São Domingos
SÃO DOMINGOS
R. QUEIRÓS
R. DOM DUARTE
R. JOÃO

IGREJA SÃO ROQUE
MUSEU DE ARTE SACRA
ROSSIO TRAIN STATION
15
ROSSIO
Rossio (Praça Dom Pedro IV)
18
Rossio
Praça da Figueira
B Bus Tours
#2, 12E & 15E
T
R. BORRATEM
28

5 BAIRRO ALTO
TR. BOA HORA
TR. AGUA FLOR
TR. DO GREMIO
TR. QUEIMADA
Largo Trindade Coelho
Largo do Cadoval
R.C. DUQUE
R. DO DUQUE
11
22
21
16
ARCH
19
BESTEGA
R. STA. JUSTA

RUA LUIZ SORIANO
RUA DA ROSA
R.S.B.VEN
7
R. DA CONDESA
R. DA OLIVIERA
R. DA TRINDADE
CONVENTO DO CARMO
ELEVADOR STA. JUSTA
BAIXA
17
RUA AUREA

TR. DOS FIEIS DE DEUS
R. NOTICIAS
R. DO NORTE
R. GAVEIA
Teatro DA TRINDADE
9
8
10
Largo do Carmo
R.D. CARMO
R. DA ASSUNÇÃO
R. DA PRATA
R. D. CORREEIROS

T. MERCES
29
R. BARROCA
T. ESPERA
6
30
31
CHIADO
R.D. CARMO
20
ARMAZÉNS DO CHIADO MALL
RUA VITORIA
RUA AUGUSTA

ELEVADOR DA BICA
R. CAL. R. LORETO
T #28E
Praça Camões
T #2BE
Baixa-Chiado
RUA GARRETT
M
Baixa-Chiado
RUA VENG
R.S. FRAN
R. DO OURO (RUA DO OURO)
R. DO CRUCIFIXO
R. DOS SAPATEIROS
R. NIC.
RUA DE

R. H. SECA
R. DA BARRO
R.ST. CAT.
Largo Barão Quintela
T.G. EMENDA
COUSSUL
SÃO CARLOS THEATER
BIBLIOTHECA PUBLICA
R. CAPELO
R. S. FINTO
Largo da Pública
RUA VENG
T #28E
RUA DE SÃO JULIÃO
RUA DE

BICA
R. ATAIDE
R. FLORES
RUA D. ALECRIM
RUA A. MARIA CARDOSO
RUA D. DE BRAGANÇA
RUA VITOR CÓRDON
C. S. FRANCISCO
Praça do Município
T #2B E
RUA DO COMÉRCIO
ARCH

RUA S. PAULO
R. NOVA DO CARVALHO
"PINK STREET" (NIGHTLIFE)
RUA DO ARSENAL
LISBON WALKER
JOSÉ I STATUE
B #794 & Aerobús #1
35

MERCADO DA RIBEIRA
R. RIBEIRA NOVA
Praça Duque de Terceira
#15E
AVE. DA RIBEIRA DAS NAUS
To Belém

CAIS DO SODRÉ TRAIN STATION
Trains to Belém, Estoril & Cascais
CAIS DO SODRÉ FERRY TERMINAL
RIVER CRUISES
To Cacilhas

1 Farol de Santa Luzia
2 A Tasquinha Rest. & Comidas de Santiago
3 Rest. Frei Papinhas
4 Restaurante Santo Antonio de Alfama
5 Rest. Bota Alta
6 A Primavera do Jerónimo & Canto do Camões Rest. & Fado

7 Cervejaria da Trindade
8 h3 Hamburgology & Food for Your Soul
9 Aqui Ha Peixe
10 Carmo Rest. & Bar
11 Café Buenos Aires
12 Buddha Sushi Buffet
13 Lost in Esplanada Bar
14 The Independent Rest.

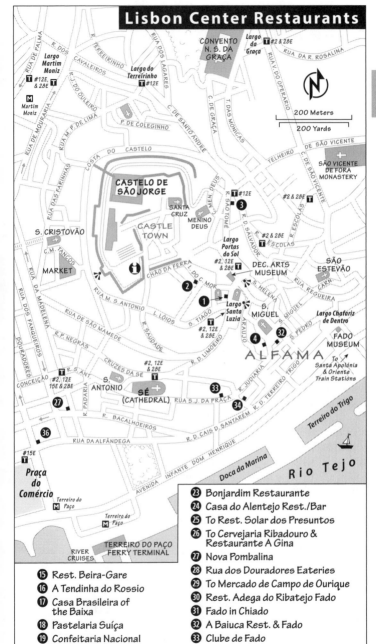

LISBON

Lisbon Center Restaurants

23 Bonjardim Restaurante
24 Casa do Alentejo Rest./Bar
25 To Rest. Solar dos Presuntos
26 To Cervejaria Ribadouro & Restaurante A Gina
27 Nova Pombalina
28 Rua dos Douradores Eateries
29 To Mercado de Campo de Ourique
30 Rest. Adega do Ribatejo Fado
31 Fado in Chiado
32 A Baiuca Rest. & Fado
33 Clube de Fado
34 Casa de Linhares Fado
35 Wines of Portugal Tasting Room
36 Martinho da Arcada Café Bar

15 Rest. Beira-Gare
16 A Tendinha do Rossio
17 Casa Brasileira of the Baixa
18 Pastelaria Suíça
19 Confeitaria Nacional
20 Armazéns do Chiado Mall
21 Rua 1 de Dezembro Eateries
22 Restaurante Leão d'Ouro

serving traditional home-style plates in a jam-packed, joyfully characteristic scene (€10-12 meals, Mon-Sat opens at 19:30, closed Sun; reserve, come early, or wait; at Travessa da Espera 38, a few steps below recommended fado place Canto do Camões, tel. 213-420-477).

IN CHIADO

Cervejaria da Trindade, a bright, boisterous, Portuguese-style beer hall, is full of historic tiles, seafood, and tourists. While over-priced and in all the guidebooks, people enjoy its atmosphere (€15-20 meals, confirm prices—especially since seafood is charged by weight, daily 12:00-24:00, liveliest 20:00-22:00, closed holidays, air-con, courtyard, a block down from São Roque Church at Rua Nova da Trindade 20-C, tel. 213-423-506).

h3 Hamburgology is a modern and trendy joint serving fancy hamburgers. Thinking out of the box, they've invented doz-ens of creative hamburger patties, all displayed with photos on the menu wall. The *menu* price includes chips, rice, and a drink for €7 (self-serve from cafeteria line, daily 12:00-23:00, Rua da Trindade 13, tel. 213-803-110). Downstairs is **Food for Your Soul,** a Wagamama-style pan-Asian eatery, handy if your soul is craving noodles.

Aqui Ha Peixe, well-lit and innovative, serves quality fish dishes under antique arches. Owner Miguel Reino insists on serv-ing only the freshest fish (€10 lunch plates, €15-22 dinner plates, Tue-Sun 12:00-15:00 & 19:00-23:00, closed Mon, Rua da Trin-dade 18A, tel. 213-432-154).

Carmo Restaurante and Bar offers tasty, light lunches in a chic but homey setting. Try a tempting dessert in one of the se-cluded back patios far away from the crowds (daily 12:00-23:00, €7 *petiscos*—snacks, Largo do Carmo 11, tel. 213-460-088).

Café Buenos Aires is a friendly place serving Argentinian cuisine (lots of red meat, €15-25 plates), hearty dinner salads, veg-etarian homemade pasta, and famous chocolate cake. Dine in the charming and intimate woody interior or at fun tables outside on a characteristic, stepped pedestrian lane (Mon-Sat 18:00-24:00, closed Sun, Rua do Duque 22, tel. 213-420-739). Above this place and on the same stepped lane are several other typically Portuguese eateries.

NEAR THE TOP OF THE ELEVADOR DA GLÓRIA FUNICULAR

Buddha Sushi Buffet has a great formula, fun energy, and handy location. While the Portuguese say *obrigado* and the Japanese say *arigato,* sushi doesn't exactly come to mind when you think about Lisbon. Still, this place serves a hearty sushi buffet for a painless price—especially if you get it to go (€8 at lunch, €11 at dinner, €4 to-go box, delightful picnic-friendly park across street, long hours daily, Rua São Pedro de Alcântara 65, mobile 964-396-927).

Lost in Esplanada Bar is understandably popular, with a Zen-like terrace, a mellow teahouse interior, a splash of Pakistan, and a view patio. The hippies who run this place brag they have the third-best view in Lisbon. They offer tasty light meals, soup, salads, and ommmm-my-goodness cocktails (closed Sun, a few blocks uphill from the funicular, at Rua D. Pedro V 56, mobile 917-759-282).

The Independente Restaurant, youthful and classy, serves modern Portuguese dishes from a creative, accessible menu to an in-the-know crowd in one big woody, candlelit ground-floor dining hall. While a bit of a splurge, it's run by a hostel (reservations smart, daily from 20:00, across from view terrace at Rua São Pedro de Alcântara 81, tel. 213-461-381).

NEAR ROSSIO
Snacks and Light Meals

The area around Rossio Station and Rossio seems designed to cater to busy locals commuting in and out by train. You'll find plenty of practical, inexpensive eateries within a block or so of the station.

Restaurante Beira-Gare is my choice for a quick, cheap meal immediately across the street from the Rossio Station. A classic greasy-spoon diner, it dishes out cod and vegetables prepared faster than a Big Mac and served with more energy than a soccer team. The house specialty is a pork sandwich *(bifana no pão)*. Consider their soup-and-sandwich special (Mon-Sat 6:00-24:00, closed Sun, stand at the bar or grab a table, Rua 1 de Dezembro, tel. 213-420-405).

A Tendinha do Rossio, established in 1840 and run by Calheiros and Carmo, is a classic cherry brandy bar that also sells soups, sandwiches, and fishy snacks. Prices are dirt-cheap and the same whether you sit with the drunks at the bar, grab a tiny table inside, or serve yourself and sit outside overlooking Rossio (Mon-Sat 7:00-21:00, closed Sun, Praça Dom Pedro IV 6, tel. 213-468-156).

Casa Brasileira of the Baixa offers a characteristic budget snack or meal in a classic local scene (daily 7:00-24:00, 100 yards from Rossio at Rua Augusta 265). Fast, cheap lunch deals are served only at the bar, or choose the sidewalk tables with a higher-priced menu. And their *pastel de nata* (custard tart), made downstairs, is as tasty as those that people line up for in Belém.

Pastelaria Suíça (SWEE-sah) provides a serviceable, air-conditioned, and comfortable place for a no-stress meal. It's popular despite its surly wait staff and relatively high prices. Along with pastry, they serve light meals, sandwiches, salads, and fruit cups (daily 7:00-21:00, least expensive at the bar, reasonable at inside tables, pricey at outside tables overlooking Rossio or Praça da Figueira, located between the two squares with entrances and terraces on each—choose sun or shade, tel. 213-214-090).

Confeitaria Nacional has been proudly satisfying sweet-tooths for 180 years, and was once the favorite of Portuguese royalty. Stop in for a tasty pastry downstairs. Or, for a peaceful and inexpensive three-course lunch, go upstairs, where you'll choose between a cheaper meal in the cafeteria or pay a little extra for service and Old World sophistication in the elegant dining room (Mon-Sat 8:00-20:00, closed Sun, Praça da Figueira 18, tel. 213-424-470 or 213-243-000).

Between Rossio and Chiado

Armazéns do Chiado Mall: This shopping center, between the Bairro Alto and the Baixa, has a sixth-floor food court offering a selection of fun eateries—mostly fast food and chain restaurants you'd find in any modern mall (daily 12:00-23:00, between Rua Garrett and Rua da Assunção; from the lower town, find the inconspicuous elevator at Rua do Crucifixo 89 or 113, next to the Baixa-Chiado Metro entrance). Some of the mall's eateries are actual restaurants with castle views. But most are fast-food joints sharing common plastic tables. **Loja das Sopas** offers hearty soups with €5 fixed-price meals and **Companhia das Sandes** offers up healthy, big-bowl pasta salads topped with tropical fruits. **Restaurant Chimarrão** serves Brazilian cuisine and offers an impressive €11 *Rodizio:* an all-you-can-eat buffet of salad, veggies, and endless beef, ham, pork, sausage, and chicken. They also have daily €7 specials, desserts, and tropical juices and fruits (tel. 213-479-444).

Rua 1 de Dezembro: This street, which is busy during the workday and dead after hours, is lined with cheap restaurants. Walk the street from Rossio Station to the Elevador de Santa Justa to determine the prevailing menu of the day. Most options are self-service, with speed being the priority for the busy office workers who eat here. The **Companhia das Sandes** sandwich shop offers salads and healthy sandwiches that you design Subway-style (daily 9:00-20:00). **Tasquinha do Celeiro** is a self-service vegetarian joint at #53. **Pingo Doce supermarket** is the only grocery store in the area (daily 8:30-21:30, at #73).

Restaurantes Leão d'Ouro is actually two restaurants set side-by-side. The basic one, with old tiles on the walls and hams hanging from the ceiling, serves decent food at fair prices. Next door its hardworking cafeteria cousin offers a cheap-and-hearty buffet with an inviting Brazilian grill all day (€7 at lunch, €9 at dinner, long hours daily, next to Rossio Station at Rua 1 de Dezembro 105, tel. 213-342-6195).

Lisbon's "Eating Lane" (North of Rossio)

Rua das Portas de Santo Antão is Lisbon's "eating lane"—a galaxy of eateries, many specializing in seafood (off the northeast corner of Rossio). While the waiters are pushy and it's all very touristy, the lane—lively with happy eaters—is enjoyable to browse. This is a fine spot to down a beer, snack on some snails, and watch people go by.

Bonjardim, a family-friendly diner on the small side street, Travessa de Santo Antão, is known for its tasty roasted chicken (paint on some spicy African *piri-piri* sauce) and fries (€10-15 per meal, daily 12:00-23:00, Travessa do Santo Antão 7 or 10, both branches run by same owner, tel. 213-427-424).

Casa do Alentejo Restaurante specializes in Alentejo cuisine and fills an old, second-floor dining hall. The Moorish-looking building is a cultural and social center for people from the traditional southern province of Portugal living in Lisbon. While the food is mainly hearty and simple, the ambience is fabulous. It's a good place to try regional specialties such as pork with clams, or the super-sweet, eggy almond dessert called *charcada*. The full-bodied Alentejo red wine is cheap and solid (€10 two-course daily lunch special, €10-15 main dishes at dinner, daily 12:00-15:00 & 19:00-22:30, slip into the closed-looking building at Rua das Portas de Santo Antão 58 and climb stairs to the right, tel. 213-469-231). They host folk dancing in the grand ballroom (often on Sat from 15:00) and ballroom dancing (on many Sun from 15:00), except in summer when it's too hot (mid-June-mid-Sept).

The **Casa do Alentejo Bar,** in the same building, serves cheap bar food and wine (same hours as restaurant, spicy meat plates, hearty cheese, other tapas; to the right of the stairs, look for Taberna sign on ground floor).

Restaurante Solar dos Presuntos keeps the theater crowd happily fed with meat and seafood specialties. Its upstairs is more elegant, while the downstairs—with a colorful, open kitchen—is higher energy. Photos of Lisbon's celebrities and politicians who eat here enliven the walls. Reservations are smart. This place can take advantage of its popularity and bulldoze tourists into spending a lot—order cautiously and know what you're paying for (€25 plates, €35-40 meals, big splittable portions, good wine list presented on an iPad, Mon-Sat 12:00-15:30 & 19:00-23:00, closed Sun, at the top end of Rua das Portas de Santo Antão at #150, tel. 213-424-253).

On Avenida da Liberdade (North of Rossio)

Cervejaria Ribadouro is a favorite splurge for locals because of its quality meat and shellfish (€15-25 meals, daily 12:00-24:00, Avenida da Liberdade 155, at intersection with Rua do Salitre, Metro:

Avenida, tel. 213-549-411). Note that seafood prices are listed by weight; the waiter will help you determine the cost of a portion. To limit the cost, write down the number of grams you want. For a fun, quick €12 per-person meal, order a small draught beer *(uma imperial)*, 100 grams (about a quarter of a pound) of *percebes* (barnacles), and *pão torrado com manteiga* (toasted bread with butter).

Restaurante A Gina, glowing like a mirage in a vacant lot that used to be a fairground, is one of my favorite places for a fine dinner in Lisbon. The cloth bibs embroidered with Gina's name indicate it's a lunchtime hit with local office workers, who appreciate the tasty traditional Portuguese grilled meat and fish. Gina and her men scramble to give this wonderful place a genuine friendliness. Two minutes off of Avenida da Liberdade (directly behind recommended Hotel Lisboa Plaza) in Parque Mayer, it feels worlds away from the tourist crowds (€10-15 plates, daily 12:00-15:00 & 18:00-24:00, reservations recommended, tel. 213-420-296). The son, Rui, speaks English. Diners with this book get a free dessert port.

Near Praça do Comércio (South of Rossio)

Nova Pombalina is a busy little joint that serves quick-fire sandwiches (€3.50), soups, and exotic fresh-squeezed juices. It's famous among office workers for its suckling pig sandwich *(sandes de leitão)*. From Praça do Comércio, it's five blocks toward the castle, on the corner of Rua do Comércio and Rua da Madalena (Rua do Comércio 2, tel. 218-874-360).

Rua dos Douradores: This street, cutting from Praça da Figueira through the Baixa, is lined with very competitive little eateries. It's fun to browse down this lane on an empty stomach. If you're craving Indian food, stop at **Restaurante Gandhi Palace,** which has a friendly Punjabi staff and nonstop Bollywood musicals on TV (€10 plates, open daily, Rua dos Douradores 214, tel. 218-873-839). They also serve Italian dishes.

MEMORABLE MARKET DINING

Mercado de Campo de Ourique is a 19th-century iron-and-glass market that has morphed into a trendy food circus (with long hours). Produce stalls, fishmongers, and bakeries (many of which close for the evening) sell everything from pigs' ears to designer cupcakes while local diners jam the place, picking up meals from whichever counter appeals and finding a place to sit in the thriving center (daily 10:00-23:00, short taxi ride or take trolley #28E to second-to-last stop: Igreja Sto. Condestável). The market is behind the big church on Campo de Ourique. (Lisbon's most interesting cemetery is one stop farther, at the end of the trolley line.)

Lisbon Connections

BY TRAIN

If leaving Lisbon by train, check to see if your train requires an advance reservation (look for a boxed "R" in the timetable). All train stations are connected to the Metro system, making departure a breeze. For snacks or train picnics, Santa Apolónia has a tightly packed Pingo Doce supermarket inside the station just past the Metro (Mon-Sat 7:30-22:00, Sun 8:30-22:00). The Vasco da Gama shopping mall next to Oriente Station has an enormous Continente supermarket below street level (Mon-Sat 9:00-24:00, Sun 9:00-13:00).

From Lisbon by Train to: Madrid (1/day, "Lusitânia" overnight 21:15-8:00, 11 hours, departs from Santa Apolónia Station, arrives at Madrid's Chamartín Station), **Paris** (1/day, overnight 21:15-18:30, 20 hours, departs Santa Apolónia, no stop in Madrid, change at Hendaye at 11:30, arrives at Paris' Gare Montparnasse), **Évora** (4/day, 1.5 hours), **Lagos** (5/day, 4 hours, departs Oriente, transfer in Tunes or Faro), **Tavira** (5/day, 4-5 hours, departs Oriente, change at Faro), **Coimbra** (almost hourly, 2 hours, departs Santa Apolónia), **Nazaré/Valado** (3-5/day, 3.5-4 hours, involves 2-3 transfers; bus is better—see below), **Óbidos** (3/day, 2.25-3 hours, transfer in Mira Sintra-Melecas or Cacém, departs Oriente), **Porto** (almost hourly, 3 hours, departs Oriente), **Sintra** (4/hour, 40 minutes, departs Rossio). For train info, call tel. 808-208-208, visit www.cp.pt, or check Germany's excellent all-Europe website, www.bahn.com. Note: Any train leaving from Santa Apolónia passes through Oriente Station a few minutes later.

To Salema: To reach Salema, you'll first need to get to **Lagos,** which is about 4 hours from Lisbon by train (see above) or bus (see below). Trains from Lisbon to the Algarve leave from Oriente Station on the Lisboa-Faro line. At Tunes, there is a transfer to a local train that takes you as far as Lagos. From there, it's a cheap bus ride or a pricier taxi ride to Salema.

BY BUS

Bus tickets to Spain are sold by InterCentro Lines in Lisbon, but the service is run by Alsa (www.alsa.es). All buses leave from Lisbon's Sete Rios bus station (Metro: Jardim Zoológico, toll tel. 707-223-344).

From Lisbon by Bus to: Coimbra (hourly, 2.5 hours), **Nazaré** (6/day, 2 hours), **Fátima** (hourly, 1.5-2.5 hours), **Batalha** (5/day, 2 hours), **Alcobaça** (6/day, 2 hours, some transfer in Caldas da Rainha), **Óbidos** (hourly, 1.25 hours, transfer in Caldas da Rainha), **Porto** (at least hourly, 3 hours), **Évora** (almost hourly, 1.5 hours), **Lagos** (5/day, 4 hours, some transfer in Albufeira, easier than train, must book ahead, get details at TI), **Tavira** (5/day direct, 4.25 hours), **Madrid** (2/day, 8-9 hours, www.avanzabus.com), **Sevilla** (2/day, 7 hours, may be less off-season; you can also get to Sevilla by taking the overnight train to Madrid, then the hourly AVE train, but the bus is your better, faster, and cheaper option).

BY PLANE

You can generally buy a plane ticket from Lisbon to Madrid on short notice for as little as €30 or as much as €300, depending on the time of year. Shop around to get the best deal. Vueling (www.vueling.com), EasyJet (www.easyjet.com), and Ryanair (www.ryanair.com) have the cheapest flights.

SINTRA

For centuries, Portugal's aristocracy considered Sintra the perfect place to escape from Lisbon. Now tourists do, too. Sintra (SEEN-trah) is a mix of natural and man-made beauty: fantasy castles set amid exotic tropical plants, lush green valleys, and craggy hilltops with hazy views of the Atlantic and Lisbon.

For centuries, Sintra—just 15 miles northwest of Lisbon—was the summer escape of Portugal's kings. Those with money and a desire to be close to royalty built their palaces amid luxuriant gardens in the same neighborhood. Lord Byron called this bundle of royal fancies and aristocratic dreams a "glorious Eden," and even though it's mobbed with tourists today, it's still magnificent. Also consider checking out Europe's westernmost tip (at Cabo da Roca) and nearby resort towns.

PLANNING YOUR TIME

Sintra makes a great day trip from Lisbon, especially on Monday, when many museums in Lisbon are closed, but all major Sintra sights are open. Here you can romp along the ruined ramparts of a deserted Moorish castle, and climb through the Versailles of Portugal—the Pena Palace—on a neighboring hilltop.

Due to its concentration of popular sights and limited public transportation, a trip to Sintra requires patience and a flexible schedule—especially when it's most crowded, from July through September. To save money, bring a picnic lunch from Lisbon and plan to eat it at the Moorish Castle or the gardens of the Pena Palace.

Try to leave Lisbon around 8:30 to arrive in Sintra by 9:15, because most major sights open between 9:30 and 9:45. Pick up

Near Lisbon

Major Train Stations
1. Santa Apolónia
2. Oriente
3. Rossio
4. Cais do Sodré

a map at the TI in Sintra's train station, and catch Scotturb bus #434 to the Moorish Castle ruins. Then catch the bus up to the Pena Palace. After touring the palace and gardens, you could catch the bus back to town (bus leaves from either castle), or you could hike 30 minutes down a steep, wooded path into town (hiking instructions marked on TI's *Parques e Palácios* map; fork in path leads down from within the castle grounds). Have lunch (unless you already had a picnic, or lunched at the Pena Palace's café), explore the town, and visit the National Palace. Then catch the train back to Lisbon in time for dinner. This general plan also works well for drivers, who ideally should leave their car in Lisbon (or at least park in Sintra) and take advantage of public transportation.

With extra time, explore the rugged and picturesque westernmost tip of Portugal at Cabo da Roca. You can also mix and mingle with the jet set—or at least press your nose against their windows—at the resort towns of Cascais or Estoril (for information on how to reach these destinations, see "Near Sintra," at the end of the chapter).

GETTING TO SINTRA

Catch the **train** to Sintra from Lisbon's central Rossio Station (direct, 4/hour, 40 minutes). The easiest way to avoid early-morning lines is to use a LisboaCard or a Viva Viagem "Zapping" card that you've charged the night before or at the nearby Restauradores Metro station. If you don't have either card, buy your ticket at Rossio Station (upstairs—at track level) from the ticket window or an automated machine (select English, then "Buy Ticket + Card," then "Stations," select "Sintra" from the list of destinations, hit "+" for return ticket, then pop in coins or small bills; €2.15 each way, no discount for round-trip, add €0.50 fee for reusable Viva Viagem card; TV monitors list departure times). Pass your card over the scanner at the turnstile to enter. Your card may eventually be checked by someone on board, and you'll need to scan it again when you leave the station in Sintra. During your ride, take in the views of the 18th-century aqueduct (on the left) and the workaday Lisbon suburbs. Relax...Sintra is at the end of the line.

Sintra is far easier by train than by **car** from Lisbon. Consider waiting until after you visit Sintra to pick up your rental car.

Orientation to Sintra

Sintra is small. The town itself sprawls at the foot of a hill, a 10-minute walk (or quick bus ride) from the train station. The National Palace, with its unmistakable pair of cone-shaped chim-

neys, is in the center of the town, a block from the TI. But the other two main sights are a steep, long, uphill walk from town; most prefer to take the bus. If you're trying to decide, look up from the train station or center of town to see the Moorish Castle wall on top of the hill—it's quite a hike even for the physically fit. The Pena Palace is beyond that.

TOURIST INFORMATION

Sintra has two TIs: a small one in the train station (tel. 219-241-623) and a larger one a block off the main square in the Museu Regional building (both open daily 10:00-18:00, until 19:00 in Aug, tel. 219-231-157, www.askmelisboa.com). Pick up a free map with information on sights and a Scotturb bus schedule. Hikers should download walking routes from the city website before arrival; the TI no longer offers printed copies (www.cm-sintra.pt). The TI can arrange *quartos* (rooms in private homes, Db-€35-80) for overnighters.

ARRIVAL IN SINTRA

By Train: Upon arrival, stop at the TI in the station. To **bus** to the town center or palace, hop on Scotturb #434 (exit station to the right to reach the nearest stop, €5 ticket valid all day, sched-

ules posted at stop; for more bus info, see "Getting Around Sintra," later). The bus stops in town first (across from the main TI) before heading up to the Pena Palace. You can also reach the town center easily on **foot** (exit station and go left; it's about a 10-minute walk filled with modern "art" and hippies selling handmade trinkets).

HELPFUL HINTS

LisboaCard: This sightseeing pass gets you discounts on the Pena Palace, Moorish Castle, National Palace, Toy Museum, and the Monserrate gardens. It also covers the train ride from Lisbon to Sintra (buy it at a Lisbon TI before you visit Sintra). Be sure to bring the LisboaCard booklet, which contains coupons required for some of the discounts.

Festivals: The Festival de Sintra music and dance festival from late May to early July keeps the town lively and fun (www.festivaldesintra.pt).

Money: ATMs are rare in Sintra. You'll find one at the train station, another inside the main TI, and one on Rua das Padarias, just up the hill from the recommended Casa Piriquita.

WCs: The only free WC in town—other than at restaurants—is located near the small, central parking lot where horse carriages also wait (Calçada do Pelourinho).

Bring a Picnic: If saving a few euros is important, buy picnic items in Lisbon. Sintra's reputation as a tourist destination means high prices for restaurant meals.

Local Guide: Christina Quental works mainly in Lisbon, but lives near Sintra and can meet you at the station (Mon-Fri €125/half-day, €195/day; mobile 919-922-480, anacristinaquental@hotmail.com).

GETTING AROUND SINTRA

Scotturb Bus #434 loops together all the important stops—the train station, the town center/TI/National Palace (stop is at TI), the Moorish Castle ruins, and the Pena Palace—before heading back to town and the train station (4/hour; schedule subject to traffic conditions; €5 ticket good all day for one loop with stops, buy from driver or Scotturb bus representative at stop near TI in town;

Sintra

ⓣ Taxi Stand   Ⓑ Bus Stop
Ⓟ Parking   → One-Way

SEE CENTRAL SINTRA MAP

N-247

TO CABO DA ROCA

CASA MIRADOURO HOTEL

TOWN HALL

#403 &
#434

ⓣ
Ⓑ

COSTA

TRAIN STATION

ESTRADA CARVAL-HEIRO

CASA DO VALLE GUESTHOUSE

NATIONAL PALACE

MAIN SQUARE

Ⓟ

ℹ

TO MONSERRATE & CABO DA ROCA

#434
Ⓑ
ⓣ

RIO DO PORTO

VOLTA DO DUCHE

LIBERDADE PARK

QUINTA DA REGALEIRA

ℹ

RUA

MAR. SALDANHA

RIBEIRO

TO LISBON
N-375

OLD TOWN

MOORISH FOUNTAIN

✝ SANTA MARIA

ESTRADA DA PENA

GREAT VIEW!

TICKET BOOTH

RUA

TRIN.

TO LISBON

MOORISH CASTLE

← TRAIL

TICKET BOOTH
MOORISH CASTLE PARKING

Ⓟ Ⓑ #434

TO TRAIN STN.

DE PENA

ESTRADA

#434

Ⓑ

LOWER PARK GATE

PENA PARK

MAIN ENTRANCE

Ⓑ
#434
TICKET BOOTH

PENA SHUTTLE TOURIST BUS

PENA PALACE

Ⓝ

DCH

100 YARDS

100 METERS

TO HIGH CROSS

first bus departs at 9:15 from train station; last bus leaves station at 19:50; entire circuit takes 30 minutes without traffic). On your way to the top of the hill, the bus will stop at the entrance to the Moorish Castle. Purchase a combo-ticket here, visiting the Moorish Castle first (because it has substantially shorter lines), then walk another 10–15 minutes—mainly uphill—to the Pena Palace (or take the bus). You can also take a **taxi** from the town center or the train station to the Moorish Castle or the Pena Palace (but it

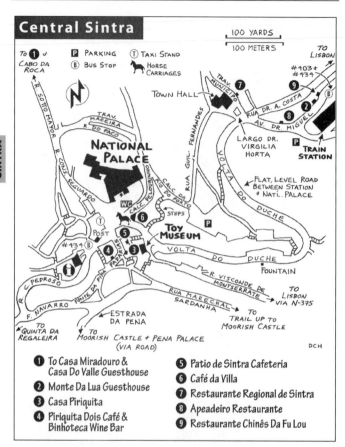

Central Sintra

100 YARDS
100 METERS

To ① ↓
CABO DA
ROCA

Ⓟ PARKING   Ⓣ TAXI STAND
Ⓑ BUS STOP   🐎 HORSE
                CARRIAGES

TO
LISBON

#403 ♦
#434

TRAV. MUNICIPIO

TOWN HALL

RUA DR. A. COSTA
AV. DR. MIGUEL

LARGO DR.
VIRGILIA
HORTA

Ⓟ TRAIN
STATION

R. SOTTO MAYOR

TRAV. MACEIRA
R. DO PAÇO

NATIONAL
PALACE

R. CONS. SEGUARDO

RUA GUIL. FERNANDES

VOLTA DO DUCHE

FLAT, LEVEL ROAD
BETWEEN STATION
& NATL. PALACE

WC

CALC. DO PELOURINHO

BECO DO PORTO

STEPS

TOY
MUSEUM

Ⓟ

POST

#434 Ⓑ

PADARIAS

VOLTA   DO   DUCHE

FOUNTAIN

R. VISCONDE DE
MONTSERRATE

TO
LISBON
VIA N-375

R. PEDROSO

FONTE DA PIPA

RUA MARECHAL
SARDANHA

TO
TRAIL UP TO
MOORISH CASTLE

R. F. NAVARRO

TO
QUINTA DA
REGALEIRA

ESTRADA
DA PENA

TO
MOORISH CASTLE & PENA PALACE
(VIA ROAD)

DCH

❶ To Casa Miradouro &
   Casa Do Valle Guesthouse
❷ Monte Da Lua Guesthouse
❸ Casa Piriquita
❹ Piriquita Dois Café &
   Binhoteca Wine Bar
❺ Patio de Sintra Cafeteria
❻ Café da Villa
❼ Restaurante Regional de Sintra
❽ Apeadeiro Restaurante
❾ Restaurante Chinês Da Fu Lou

won't get you any closer to the palace entrance than the bus). From the Pena Palace, wait for a bus returning to town. If there are too many people in line, backtrack downhill to the Moorish Castle for practically no wait (return to the bus-and-taxi stop, then follow signs down road to the *Moorish Castle* or walk through the forest following *Canopy Sintra* signs).

The clip-clop **horse carriages** cost about €30 for 25 minutes (rates posted). They can take you anywhere; you'll likely see them waiting by the parking lot just in front of the National Palace.

Sights in Sintra

▲Moorish Castle (Castelo dos Mouros)

Sintra's thousand-year-old ruins of a Moorish castle are lost in an enchanted forest and alive with winds of the past. They're a castle lover's dream come true, and a great place for a picnic with a panoramic Atlantic view. Though built by the Moors, the castle was taken by Christian forces in 1147. What you'll climb on today—while dramatic—was significantly restored in the 19th century. The Moorish Castle, with its own bus #434 stop, is a steep 30-minute hike from town, and a 10- to 15-minute hike from the Pena Palace's main entrance.

SINTRA

Cost and Hours: Castle-€7.50, combo-ticket with Pena Palace and gardens-€18, daily 9:30-20:00, last entry one hour before closing, free map includes English info and detailed map, tel. 219-237-300, www.parquesdesintra.pt.

Getting In: If the ticket booth near the bus stop is crowded, head to the ticket booth inside the castle at the innermost gate, which typically has little or no wait. Purchase your combo-ticket here to save time at the Pena Palace.

▲▲Pena Palace (Palácio de Pena)

This magical hilltop palace sits high above Sintra, above the Moorish Castle ruins. In the 19th century, Portugal had a very romantic prince, German-born Prince Ferdinand. A contemporary

and cousin of Bavaria's "Mad" King Ludwig (of Disneyesque Neuschwanstein Castle fame), Ferdinand was also a cousin of England's Prince Albert (Queen Victoria's husband). Flamboyant Ferdinand hired a German architect to build a fantasy castle, mixing elements of German and Portuguese style. He ended up with a crazy Neo-fortified casserole of Gothic towers, Renaissance domes, Moorish minarets, Manueline carvings, Disney playfulness, and an *azulejo* (tile) toilet for his wife.

Cost and Hours: Palace and gardens-€14, combo-ticket with Moorish Castle-€18, daily May-mid-Sept 9:45-19:00, last entry 45 minutes before closing, tel. 219-105-340, www.parquesdesintra.pt.

Getting In: Purchase your ticket at the small hut next to the gated main entrance. To avoid the 10-minute uphill climb from the entrance to the palace (and enjoy a lift back down), catch the green shuttle bus just inside the gate at the *paragem* sign (€3 round-trip, purchase ticket inside gift shop—*not* from driver, departs about every 10 minutes).

Information: English descriptions throughout the palace give meaning to the rooms. Your ticket also comes with a map showing a circular, 1.5-hour walking route of the park. Be sure to grab the English version of this map if you intend to explore the park after touring the palace.

Eating: The palace has a view café. If you brought your lunch with you, enjoy it in the picnic-perfect gardens either before or after your visit. Wander in, find a spot of shade, and enjoy views fit for a king.

◑ Visiting the Palace: The palace, built in the mid- to late 1800s, is so well-preserved that it feels as if it's the day after the royal family fled Portugal in 1910 (during a popular revolt that eventually made way for today's modern republic). This gives the place a charming intimacy rarely seen in palaces. Here are the highlights.

Entry: After you hop off the green shuttle bus, walk up through the Moorish archway with alligator decor. Keep your ticket handy because it will be checked several times during the visit. Cross the drawbridge that doesn't draw, and join an onion-domed world of tourists frozen in deep knee-bends with their cameras cocked. At the base of the stairs, you'll see King Ferdinand, who built this castle from 1840 until 1885, when he died. Though German, he was a romantic proponent of his adopted culture and did much to preserve Portugal's architectural and artistic heritage.

Courtyard: The palace was built on the site of a 16th-century monastery; the courtyard was the former location of the cloister. In spite of its plushness, the palace retains the monkish coziness of several small rooms gathered in two levels around the cloister.

Like its big brother in Belém, the monastery housed followers of St. Jerome, the hermit monk. Like their namesake, the monks wanted to be isolated, and this was about as isolated as you could be around here 500 years ago. The spot was also a popular pilgrimage destination for its statue of "Our Lady of the Feathers" (*pena* means feather—hence the palace's name). In 1498 King Manuel was up here enjoying the view when he spied Vasco da Gama sailing up the river, returning safely from his great voyage. To celebrate and give thanks, the king turned what was a humble wooden monastery into a fine stone palace.

Dining Room and Pantry: Stuck into a cozy corner, the monastery's original refectory was decked out with the royal family's finest tableware and ceiling tiles.

Workshop of King Charles (Carlos I): With a shaky empire crumbling around him, King Charles found refuge in art—specifically the latest style, Art Nouveau. Unfinished paintings and sketches eerily predict the king's unfinished rule.

King's Bedroom: The king enjoyed cutting-edge comforts, including the shower/tub imported from England, and even a telephone to listen to the opera when he couldn't face the Lisbon commute. The bedroom is decorated in classic Romantic style—dark, heavy, and crowded with knickknacks.

Queen's Bedroom and Dressing Room: Study the melancholy photos of Queen Amelia (Amélie of Orléans), King Charles, and their family in this room. The early 1900s were a rocky time for Portugal's royal family. The king and his eldest son were assassinated in 1908. His youngest son, Manuel II, became king until he, his mother the queen, and other members of the royal family fled Portugal during the 1910 revolution. The palm frond on the headboard of the queen's bed was from her last Palm Sunday Mass in Portugal. Poke around. Throughout the palace, you'll see state-of-the-art conveniences (the first flush toilets and hot shower in Portugal). The whole place is lovingly cluttered, typical of the Victorian horror of empty spaces.

Queen's View Balcony: On the upper floor, enjoy a sweeping view from Lisbon to the mouth of the Rio Tejo. Find the Cristo Rei statue and the 25th of April Bridge. The statue on the distant ridge honors the palace's architect.

The New Wing: This spacious addition to the original series of rooms around the cloister includes the apartments of the last king and the fantastically furnished Noble's Room.

End of Palace Tour: Your tour ends at the abundant kitchen; just after, a view café conveniently welcomes us peasants. After touring the palace, you can return directly to the main entrance (walk 10 minutes or catch the green shuttle bus—your ticket covers the round-trip), or you can detour for a self-guided tour of the park.

Chapel: Wander through the inner patio to find a pointed dome covered in green and white tiles. Climb the steps to visit the royal family's sumptuous private chapel decorated in a variety of styles. The structure is Manueline, reminiscent of the Monastery of Jerónimos in Belém.

Pena Palace Park: The lush, captivating, and sprawling palace grounds, rated ▲, are dotted with romantic surprises, including the High Cross (highest point around, with commanding views), chapels, a temple, lakes, giant sequoia trees, and exotic plants. If you want to walk through the park after you tour the palace, take a 30- to 40-minute stroll downhill (following the *Parques e Palácios* map that came with your palace admission) to the lower park gate, where you'll find a bus stop and the Estrada de Pena loop road.

SINTRA

From here, it's a five-minute hike uphill to the Moorish Castle, or a ten-minute hike up to the Pena Palace's main entrance.

▲▲National Palace (Palácio Nacional)

While the palace dates back to Moorish times, most of what you'll see is from the 15th-century reign of King John (João) I, with later Manueline architectural ornamentation from the 16th century.

This oldest surviving royal palace in Portugal is still used for official receptions. Having housed royalty for 500 years (until 1910), it's fragrant with history.

Cost and Hours: €9.50, daily 9:30-19:00, last entry 18:30; look for white, Madonna-bra building in town center, 10-minute walk from train station, photos allowed, tel. 219-237-300, www.parquesdesintra.pt.

➋ Visiting the Palace: The palace is a one-way romp with little information provided. As you tour the place, stop in these notable parts of the palace:

Swan Room: This first room is the palace's banquet room. A king's daughter—who loved swans—married into a royal house in Belgium. The king missed the princess so much that he decorated the ceiling with her favorite animal. These aren't the only creatures in the room, though. Check out the ceramic soup tureens designed in the shape of your favorite barnyard animal.

Courtyard: This was a fortified medieval palace, so rather than having fancy gardens outside, it has a stay-awhile courtyard within its protective walls. Notice the unique chimneys. They provide powerful suction that removes the smoke from the kitchen and also create a marvelous open-domed feeling (as you'll see at the end of your tour).

Magpie Room: King John I was caught kissing a lady-in-waiting by his queen. Frustrated by his court—abuzz with gossip—John had this ceiling painted with magpies. But to show what a good-spirited guy he was, around each magpie is the king's slogan—*Por bem*, "For good." The 15th-century Moorish tiles are from Spain, brought in before the development of the famous, ubiquitous Portuguese tiles, and are considered some of the finest Moorish-Spanish tiles in all of Iberia.

King's Bedroom: The king portrayed on the wall where you enter the room is King Sebastian (Dom Sebastião), a gung-ho, medieval-type monarch who went to battle in Africa, following the Moors even after they were chased out of Europe. He disap-

SINTRA

peared in 1578 at age 24 (although he was almost certainly killed in Morocco, "Sebastianists" awaited his mythical return into the 19th century). With the king missing, Portugal was left in unstable times with only Sebastian's great uncle (King Henrique) as heir. The new king died within two years, and the throne passed to his great uncle, King Philip II of Spain, leading to 60 years of Spanish rule (1580-1640).

Note the ebony, silver, and painted copper headboard of the Italian Renaissance bed. The tiles in this room are considered the first Portuguese tiles—from the time of Manuel I. The corn-on-the-cob motif topping the tilework is a reminder of American discoveries. Wander through more rooms upstairs, and through more quarters to the blue-and-gold...

Stag Room: The most striking room in the palace honors Portugal's loyal nobility. Study the richly decorated ceiling. The king's coat of arms at the top is surrounded by the coats of arms of his children, and below that, the coats of arms of all but one of Portugal's noble families (the omitted family had schemed a revolt, so received only a blank niche). The Latin phrase circling the room reads, "Honoring all the noble families who've been loyal to the king." The 18th-century tiles hang from the walls like tapestries. Enjoy the view: a garden-like countryside dotted with mansions of nobility who clamored to be near their king, the hill-capping castle, and the wide-open Atlantic. You're in the westernmost room of the westernmost palace on the European continent.

Kitchen: With all the latest in cooking technology, the palace chef could roast an entire cow on the spit, keep the king's plates warm in the iron dish warmer (with drawers below for the charcoal), and get really dizzy by looking up and spinning around three times. OK, you can go now.

▲Quinta da Regaleira

This Neo-everything (Manueline/Gothic/Renaissance) 1912 mansion and garden has mystical and Masonic twists. It was designed by an Italian opera-set designer for a wealthy but disgruntled monarchist two years after the royal family was deposed. The two-hour English tour is mostly in the garden (as the palace is quite small) and can be longish unless you're into quirky Masonic esoterica. If you like fantastic caves, bring a flashlight and follow the shaded black lines on the provided maps. Ask a local to pronounce "Regaleira" for you, and just try to repeat it.

Cost and Hours: €6 self-guided tour, €10 guided tour by reservation only, 7 tours daily April-Sept, fewer off-season; open daily 10:00-20:00, closes earlier off-season, last entry one hour before closing; 10-minute walk from downtown Sintra, café; book tours online at www.regaleira.pt or by calling 219-106-650.

Toy Museum (Museu do Brinquedo)

Just for giggles, you can wander through a collection of several thousand old-time toys, from small soldiers, planes, cars, trucks, and old tricycles to a dolls' attic upstairs. The 20th-century owner, João Arbués Moreira, started collecting toys when he was 14 and never quit. The collection is displayed in chronological order and comes with no English descriptions. Moreira typically hangs around the museum in his wheelchair, and loves to explain to visitors how he acquired each item.

Cost and Hours: €5, €3 for those under 19, Tue-Sun 10:00-18:00, closed Mon, last entry 30 minutes before closing, kids' play zone, one block in front of National Palace on Rua Visconde de Monserrate 26, tel. 219-242-171, www.museu-do-brinquedo.pt.

Monserrate

About 2.5 miles outside of Sintra are the wonderful gardens of Monserrate. If you like tropical plants and exotic landscaping, a visit is time well-spent, though many find that the Pena Palace's gardens are just as good as these more famous grounds.

Cost and Hours: €7.50, €5 extra for guided visit by reservation only, daily 9:30-20:00 last entry one hour before closing, no buses run here—allow about €10 for taxi, tel. 219-237-300, www.parquesdesintra.pt.

Sleeping in Sintra

$$ Casa Miradouro is a beautifully restored mansion from 1893. With eight spacious, stylish rooms, an elegant lounge, castle and sea views, and a wonderful garden, it's a worthy splurge (Db-€95-135, less Nov-March, includes buffet breakfast, Wi-Fi, street parking, Rua Sotto Major 55; from National Palace, go past Hotel Tivoli Sintra and 400 yards downhill, note that it's a stiff uphill hike to return to center; mobile 914-292-203, www.casa-miradouro.com, mail@casa-miradouro.com, Charlotte Lambregts).

$$ Casa Do Valle Guesthouse offers seven comfortable, modern rooms in a peaceful location. They have a lovely garden and large deck with valley and castle views (Db-€80-120, less Nov-March, breakfast-€4-6, guest computer, Wi-Fi, pool, street parking, behind Casa Miradouro on Rua da Paderna LT-2, tel. 219-244-699, www.casadovalle.com, info@casadovalle.com).

$ Monte Da Lua Guesthouse has seven clean, simple, fine rooms with shiny hardwood floors, facing the train station (one D-€55-60, six Db-€55-70, highest price is for July-Aug, 5 percent discount if you pay cash and mention this book, no breakfast, Wi-Fi, Avenida Dr. Miguel Bombarda 51, tel. 219-241-029, www.montedalua.org, montedalua51@gmail.com, Silvia).

Sleep Code

Abbreviations   (€1 = about $1.40, country code: 351)
S = Single, **D** = Double/Twin, **T** = Triple, **Q** = Quad, **b** = bathroom, **s** = shower only.
Price Rankings
  $$ Higher Priced—Most rooms €80 or more.
   $ Lower Priced—Most rooms less than €80.
Unless otherwise noted, credit cards are accepted, English is spoken, breakfast is included, and Wi-Fi is generally free. Prices change; verify current rates online or by email. For the best prices, always book directly with the hotel.

Eating in Sintra

LIGHT MEALS
On Rua das Padarias
This touristy little cobbled lane is lined with charming shops and eateries. While there are plenty of appealing options, here are three notable choices:

Casa Piriquita bills itself as "the" *antiga fabrica de queijadas*—historic maker of tiny, tasty tarts with a cheesy filling. It's good for a sweet and a coffee or a simple lunch, such as toasted sandwiches. Take a seat in the café (up a few steps) to avoid groups who rush in to get pastries to go, or do battle and grab a half-dozen for €4.40 (daily 8:30-22:00, Rua das Padarias 1 at the base of the street, tel. 219-230-626).

Piriquita Dois, sister to Casa Piriquita, is a block farther up the lane and may have less commotion. It has a more extensive menu and a view terrace (same hours and phone as Casa Piriquita, Rua das Padarias 18).

Binhoteca, a welcoming little *enoteca*, provides wine-lovers with an astonishing array of Portuguese wines and ports available by the glass (€2-6 and way up), along with tasty meat-and-cheese plates and a knowledgeable staff happy to explain what you're enjoying (daily 12:00-22:00, Rua das Padarias 16, tel. 219-240-849).

More Light Choices
Patio de Sintra Cafeteria is a practical lunch stop just a block off Rua das Padarias (Rua Arco do Teixeira 15).

Café da Villa, a favorite of bus drivers and tour guides, offers generous portions of homemade-style soups and salads in a homey pub-like setting. It's good for a quiet, inexpensive lunch (€8 fixed-price meals, daily 12:00-24:00, down the road past horse-drawn carriages at Calçada do Pelourinho 2, tel. 219-241-174).

Pizza Hut, at the #434 bus stop outside the train station, has a salad bar and to-go boxes for a cheap meal to munch in the Pena Palace Park, on the grounds of the Moorish Castle, or on the train ride back to Lisbon (daily 12:00-23:00, Avenida Dr. Miguel Bombarda, Edifício Grande Velocidade, tel. 707-211-122).

DINING

While there are plenty of tourist eateries in Sintra's old center, I'd head a couple of blocks away to the station area for a serious meal.

Restaurante Regional de Sintra, which feeds locals and tourists very well, is my favorite place for dinner in Sintra. Gentle Paulo speaks English and serves huge, splittable portions (€15 *doses,* daily 12:00-16:00 & 19:00-22:30, 200 yards from train station at Travessa do Municipio 2; exit train station left, go downhill to the first square and to the far-right corner; tel. 219-234-444).

Apeadeiro Restaurante, named for the platform along the track at the train station just a block away, is a quality eatery serving good food at good prices. Their daily specials can be split, allowing two to eat for €15 (Fri-Wed 9:00-24:00, closed Thu, Avenida Dr. Miguel Bombarda 3, tel. 219-231-804).

Restaurante Chinês Da Fu Lou, across the street from the train station, offers decent, affordable Chinese food and an alternative to *bacalhau* and sandwiches (€5-10 entrées, daily 11:00-15:00 & 17:00-23:00, Avenida Dr. Miguel Bombarda 53, tel. 219-242-653).

Sintra Connections

From Sintra by Train and Bus to: Lisbon (4 trains/hour, 40 minutes), **Cascais** (8 buses/day, fewer on weekends, bus #403 also stops at Cabo da Roca and the Cascais train station, 45-60 minutes, catch bus at the Sintra train station).

ROUTE TIPS FOR DRIVERS

Sintra Day Trip from Lisbon: If you insist on taking a car to Sintra, take the IC-19 freeway out of Lisbon (allow 30 minutes). When you arrive in Sintra, follow *Centro Histórico* signs. Cars are the curse of Sintra—traffic can be terrible and parking difficult. Park your car and use bus #434 to get around. There's a strip of parking along Volta do Duche, near the town center (€0.50/hour, 4-hour maximum), and a small lot next to the train station. The most central free parking lot is on Rua do Porto in the valley just below and northeast of town (after parking, climb the long set of steps to get up to the main square). If you decide (probably regrettably) to drive to the sights, you'll take a one-way winding loop—park as soon as you can, or you'll risk having to drive the huge loop again (because you can't backtrack). Large monitors can be found near every lot describing the current parking situation—most likely *completo*.

Loop Trip: It's possible to make a 70-mile circular trip and drive to all the destinations near Lisbon within a day (Lisbon–Belém–Sintra–Cabo da Roca–Cascais–Lisbon), but traffic congestion around Sintra, especially on weekends and during rush hour, can mess up your schedule.

Continuing to the Algarve: Drivers eager for beach time can leave Lisbon, visit Sintra, then head back south to drive directly to the Algarve that evening (4 hours from Lisbon). To get to the Algarve from Sintra/Cascais, get on the freeway heading for Lisbon and exit at the *Sul Ponte A-2* sign, which takes you over the 25th of April Bridge and south on A-2.

Near Sintra

The following sights are worth considering if you have extra time. They're tourable by car or by public transportation (bus and train).

If you're bent on seeing sights west of Lisbon (Sintra, Cabo da Roca, Cascais, and/or Estoril) in a long day using public transportation, consider this slam-bam swing around the peninsula: Start at the Sintra train station and buy a day pass for the Scotturb **bus** (€12). Use the pass to take bus #434 to Sintra's sights, then go to Cabo da Roca on bus #403 (see next). Next, catch the next bus #403 for the jaunt to Cascais and a seafood dinner on the waterfront.

From Cascais, returning to Lisbon is a snap—just buy a one-way **train** ticket to Lisbon at the train station. You'll get off at the last stop on the line (Cais de Sodré Station), a five-minute walk from Praça do Comércio in downtown Lisbon.

Estoril is a short train ride away on the same line to Lisbon, but seeing both Cascais and Estoril is probably redundant, and Cascais is more appealing.

Cabo da Roca

Wind-beaten, tourist-infested Cabo da Roca is the westernmost point in Europe, perhaps the inspiration for the Portuguese poet Luís de Camões' line, *"Onde a terra se acaba e o mar começa"* ("Where land ends and the sea begins"). It has a little shop, a café, and a tiny **TI** that sells an expensive €11 "proof of being here" certificate. Take a photo instead (daily May-Sept 9:00-20:00, until 19:00 off-

season, tel. 219-280-801). Nearby, on the road to Cascais, you'll pass a good beach for wind, waves, sand, and the chance to be the last person in Europe to see the sun set. For a remote beach, drive to Praia Adraga (north of Cabo da Roca).

Cascais and Estoril

Before the rise of the Algarve, these towns were the haunt of Portugal's rich and beautiful. Today, they are quietly elegant, with noble old buildings, beachfront promenades, a bullring, a casino, and more fame than they deserve. Cascais (kahsh-KAH-eesh; see photo) is the more enjoyable of the two; it's not as rich and stuffy, and it has the cozy touch of a fishing village, great seafood, and a younger, less pretentious atmosphere. The

TIs share the same hours (Mon-Fri 10:00-18:00, Sat-Sun 14:00-18:00; Cascais TI at Visconde de Luz 14, tel. 214-822-327, www. cm-cascais.pt; Estoril TI at Areada do Parque, tel. 214-663-813). Bullfight fans could enjoy a bullfight—if one is scheduled—in either city (ask at the TI).

Both towns are a simple day trip from Lisbon (4 trains/hour, 30 minutes from Lisbon's Cais do Sodré Station).

PRACTICALITIES

This section covers just the basics on traveling in Portugal (for much more information, see *Rick Steves Portugal*). You can find free advice on specific topics at www.ricksteves.com/tips.

Money

Portugal uses the euro currency: 1 euro (€) = about $1.40. To convert prices in euros to dollars, add about 40 percent: €20 = about $28, €50 = about $70. (Check www.oanda.com for the latest exchange rates.)

The standard way for travelers to get euros is to withdraw money from ATMs (which locals call *caixa eletrônico*) using a debit or credit card. Before departing, call your bank or credit-card company: Confirm that your card(s) will work overseas, ask about international transaction fees, and alert them that you'll be making withdrawals in Europe. Visa-brand cards work best. Some readers report having difficulty using MasterCard-brand debit cards at Portugal's hotels, restaurants, and ATMs, even when they've notified their bank ahead of time. For the best chances of accessing money from your US bank account, look for an ATM that uses a network whose logo is on the back of your ATM card (for example, Cirrus or Accel). Note that in Portugal, the maximum you can withdraw per transaction is €200.

Also ask for the PIN number for your credit card in case it'll help you use Europe's "chip-and-PIN" payment machines (see below); allow time for your bank to mail your PIN to you. Memorizing your credit card's PIN lets you use it at some chip-and-PIN machines—just enter your PIN when prompted. To keep your valuables safe, wear a money belt.

Dealing with "Chip and PIN": Much of Europe—including Portugal—has shifted to a "chip-and-PIN" security system for credit and debit cards, and some merchants rely on it exclusively. (European chip-and-PIN cards are embedded with an electronic security chip, and require the purchaser to punch in a PIN rather than sign a receipt.) If you happen to encounter chip and PIN, it will probably be at payment machines, such as those at train stations, toll roads, or self-serve gas pumps. On the outside chance that a machine won't take your card, don't panic. Find a cashier who can make your card work (they can print a receipt for you to sign), or find a machine that takes cash. You can always use an ATM to withdraw cash with your magnetic-stripe card, even in countries where people predominantly use chip-and-PIN cards.

Phoning

Smart travelers use the telephone to reserve or reconfirm rooms, reserve restaurants, get directions, research transportation connections, confirm tour times, phone home, and lots more.

To call Portugal from the US or Canada: Dial 011-351 and then the local number. (The 011 is our international access code, and 351 is Portugal's country code.)

To call Portugal from a European country: Dial 00-351 followed by the local number. (The 00 is Europe's international access code.)

To call within Portugal: Just dial the local number.

To call from Portugal to another country: Dial 00 followed by the country code (for example, 1 for the US or Canada), then the area code and number. If you're calling European countries whose phone numbers begin with 0, you'll usually have to omit that 0 when you dial.

Tips on Phoning: A mobile phone—whether an American one that works in Portugal, or a European one you buy when you arrive—is handy, but can be pricey. If traveling with a smartphone, consider getting an international plan from your provider and try to switch off data-roaming until you have free Wi-Fi. With Wi-Fi, you can use your smartphone to make free or inexpensive domestic and international calls by taking advantage of a calling app such as Skype, FaceTime, or Google+ Hangouts.

To make cheap international calls while in Portugal from any phone (even your hotel-room phone), you can buy an international phone card (called a *cartão telefónico com código pessoal*). These cards work with a scratch-to-reveal PIN code at any phone, allow you to call home to the US for pennies a minute, and also work for domestic calls within Portugal.

Another option is buying an insertable, electronic chip card (called a *cartão telefónico*). These are usable only at pay phones, are reasonable for making calls within Portugal (and work for international calls as well, though not as cheaply as the international phone cards). Note that insertable phone cards—and most international phone cards—only work in the country where you buy them.

From:	rick@ricksteves.com
Sent:	Today
To:	info@hotelcentral.com
Subject:	Reservation request for 19-22 July

Dear Hotel Central,

I would like to reserve a room for 2 people for 3 nights, arriving 19 July and departing 22 July. If possible, I would like a quiet room with a double bed and a bathroom inside the room.

Please let me know if you have a room available and the price.

Thank you!
Rick Steves

Calling from your hotel-room phone is usually expensive, unless you use an international phone card. For much more on phoning, see www.ricksteves.com/phoning.

Making Hotel Reservations

To ensure the best value, I recommend reserving rooms in advance, particularly during peak season. Email the hotelier with the following key pieces of information: number and type of rooms; number of nights; date of arrival; date of departure; and any special requests. (For a sample form, see the sidebar.) Use the European style for writing dates: day/month/year. Hoteliers typically ask for your credit-card number as a deposit.

Given the economic downturn, hoteliers may be willing to make a deal—try emailing several hotels to ask their best price. In general, hotel prices can soften if you do any of the following: offer to pay cash, stay at least three nights, or travel off-season.

Eating

The Portuguese meal schedule is slightly later than in the US. Their breakfast *(pequeno almoço)* is just coffee and a sweet roll. Lunch *(almoço)* is the big meal, served between 12:30 and 14:00, while supper *(jantar)* is from about 19:30 to 21:30. All restaurants are smoke-free to meet EU regulations.

Eat fresh seafood in Portugal, except on Monday, when the fish isn't fresh. Cod *(bacalhau)* is a mainstay, but definitely an acquired taste. Fish soup *(sopa de peixe)* and shellfish soup *(sopa de mariscos)* are worth seeking out. *Cataplana* is a delicious mix of seafood and potatoes cooked in a copper clamshell dish. The "Portuguese paella" is *arroz de mariscos,* seafood stew with rice. *Carne de porco á Alentejana* is an interesting combination of pork and clams. *Caldo verde* is a popular vegetable soup. *Frango assado* is roast chicken; ask for *piri-piri* sauce if you like it hot and spicy.

At a restaurant, be warned that if the waiter brings you appetizers you didn't order (such as olives, bread, or pâtés), it is not free. If you don't want it, push it to the side—you won't be charged for what you don't touch. But taking just one olive means you pay for the whole dish.

Many restaurants save their customers money by portioning their dishes for two people. Menus often list prices for entrées in two columns: *dose* and *meia dose*. A *dose* is generally enough to feed two, while a *meia dose* is a half-portion (plenty for one person). Restaurants have absolutely no problem with diners splitting a single *dose*. *Prato do dia* is the daily special.

Service: When you want the bill, say, *"A conta, por favor."* Most restaurants include a service charge in their prices (check the menu for *serviço incluido*). To reward very good service, you can leave a tip of up to 5 percent; if service is not included *(serviço não incluido),* tip up to 10 percent. Leave the tip on the table. It's best to tip in cash, even if you pay with your credit card. If you order your food at a counter, don't tip.

Transportation

By Train and Bus: Portugal straggles behind the rest of Europe in train service, but offers excellent bus transportation. The best public transportation option is to mix bus and train travel; because of this, the country railpass—the Portugal Pass—is generally not a good value. If you're traveling beyond Portugal, the Spain-Portugal Pass or Select Eurail pass can make sense, but use the pass wisely, just for your long train trips (for prices and specifics, visit www.ricksteves.com/rail). To research train schedules, see Portugal's train website (www.cp.pt, includes Spain and France connections) or Germany's excellent all-Europe website (www.bahn.com).

Portugal has a number of different bus companies, sometimes running buses to the same destinations and using the same transfer points. If you have to transfer, make sure to look for a bus with the same name/logo as the company you bought the ticket from. The largest national company is Rede Expressos (covers buses both north and south of Lisbon, www.rede-expressos.pt).

By Car: It's cheaper to arrange most car rentals from the US. For tips on your insurance options, see www.ricksteves.com/cdw, and for route planning, consult www.viamichelin.com. Bring your driver's license. Portugal is statistically one of Europe's most dangerous places to drive. If you're starting your trip in big-city Lisbon, don't rent a car until you're on your way out (and consider renting from the airport location). Note that it's simpler to day-trip to Sintra by train rather than by car.

Superhighways come with tolls, but save huge amounts of

time if you're crossing the country. For some toll roads, you pick up a ticket as you enter. Other roads are tolled electronically using cameras, which identify cars by their license plate and charge the appropriate fees via a simple electronic payment system. Ask your rental agency about this toll system.

Be sure all of your valuables are out of sight and locked in the trunk, or even better, with you or in your hotel room. Local road etiquette is similar to that in the US. Ask your car-rental company about the rules of the road, or check the US State Department website (www.travel.state.gov, click on "International Travel," then specify your country of choice and click "Traffic Safety and Road Conditions").

Helpful Hints

Emergency Help: For English-speaking police or an ambulance, dial 112. For passport problems, call the US Embassy (in Lisbon—tel. 217-273-300, http://portugal.usembassy.gov).

If you have a minor illness, do as the locals do and go to a pharmacist for advice. Or ask at your hotel for help—they know of the nearest medical and emergency services. For other concerns, get advice from your hotelier.

Theft or Loss: While the city is generally safe, if you're looking for trouble—especially after dark—you may find it. Pickpockets target tourists on popular trolley routes and the Metro. Don't believe any "police officers" looking for counterfeit bills. Enjoy the sightseeing, but be aware of your surroundings—wear your money belt and keep your pack zipped up.

To replace a passport, you'll need to go in person to an embassy (see above). Cancel and replace your credit and debit cards by calling these 24-hour US numbers collect: Visa—tel. 303/967-1096, MasterCard—tel. 636/722-7111, American Express—tel. 336/393-1111. In Portugal, to make a collect call to the US, dial 800-800-128; press zero or stay on the line for an operator. File a police report either on the spot or within a day or two; it's required if you submit an insurance claim for lost or stolen rail passes or electronics, and it can help with replacing your passport or credit and debit cards. Precautionary measures can minimize the effects of loss—back up your digital photos and other files frequently. For more information, see www.ricksteves.com/help.

Time: Portugal uses the 24-hour clock. It's the same through 12:00 noon, then keep going: 13:00, 14:00, and so on. Portugal's time zone is the same as Great Britain's: generally five/eight hours ahead of the East/West Coasts of the US.

Business Hours: Some businesses in Portugal take an afternoon break (about 13:00–15:00). Small shops are usually open on Saturday only in the morning and are closed all day Sunday. Banks are generally open Monday through Friday from 8:30 to 15:00.

Dress Code: At churches, a modest dress code (no bare shoulders or shorts) is encouraged.

Holidays and Festivals: Europe celebrates many holidays, which can close sights and attract crowds (book hotel rooms ahead). For information on holidays and festivals in Portugal, check the country's website: www.visitportugal.com. For a simple list showing major—though not all—events, see www.ricksteves.com/festivals.

Numbers and Stumblers: What Americans call the second floor of a building is the first floor in Europe. Europeans write dates as day/month/year, so Christmas 2016 is 25/12/16. Commas are decimal points and vice versa—a dollar and a half is 1,50, and there are 5.280 feet in a mile. Portugal uses the metric system: A kilogram is 2.2 pounds; a liter is about a quart; and a kilometer is six-tenths of a mile.

Resources from Rick Steves

This Snapshot guide is excerpted from the latest edition of *Rick Steves Portugal,* which is one of more than 30 titles in my series of guidebooks on European travel. I also produce a public television series, *Rick Steves' Europe,* and a public radio show, *Travel with Rick Steves.* My website, www.ricksteves.com, offers free travel information, a forum for travelers' comments, guidebook updates, my travel blog, an online travel store, and information on European rail passes and our tours of Europe. If you're bringing a mobile device on your trip, you can download free information from *Rick Steves Audio Europe,* featuring podcasts of my radio shows, free audio tours of major sights in Europe, and travel interviews about Portugal (via www.ricksteves.com/audioeurope, iTunes, Google Play, or the Rick Steves Audio Europe free smartphone app). You can follow me on Facebook and Twitter.

Additional Resources

Tourist Information: www.visitlisboa.com and www.visitportugal.com
Passports and Red Tape: www.travel.state.gov
Packing List: www.ricksteves.com/packing
Cheap Flights: www.kayak.com
Airplane Carry-on Restrictions: www.tsa.gov/travelers
Updates for This Book: www.ricksteves.com/update

How Was Your Trip?

If you'd like to share your tips, concerns, and discoveries after using this book, please fill out the survey at www.ricksteves.com/feedback. Thanks in advance—it helps a lot.

PRACTICALITIES

Portuguese Survival Phrases

In the phonetics, nasalized vowels are indicated by an underlined **n** or **w**. As you say the vowel, let its sound come through your nose as well as your mouth.

English	Portuguese	Pronunciation
Good day.	*Bom dia.*	boh<u>n</u> **dee**-ah
Do you speak English?	*Fala inglês?*	**fah**-lah een-**glaysh**
Yes. / No.	*Sim. / Não.*	seeng / no<u>w</u>
I (don't) understand.	*(Não) compreendo.*	(no<u>w</u>) koh<u>n</u>-pree-**ay<u>n</u>**-doo
Please.	*Por favor.*	poor fah-**vor**
Thank you. (said by male)	*Obrigado.*	oo-bree-**gah**-doo
Thank you. (said by female)	*Obrigada.*	oo-bree-**gah**-dah
I'm sorry.	*Desculpe.*	dish-**kool**-peh
Excuse me (to pass).	*Com licença.*	koh<u>n</u> li-**sehn**-sah
(No) problem.	*(Não) há problema.*	(no<u>w</u>) ah proo-**blay**-mah
Good.	*Bom.*	boh<u>n</u>
Goodbye.	*Adeus. / Ciao.*	ah-**deh**-oosh / chow
one / two	*um / dois*	oo<u>n</u> / doysh
three / four	*três / quatro*	traysh / **kwah**-troo
five / six	*cinco / seis*	**seeng**-koo / saysh
seven / eight	*sete / oito*	**seh**-teh / **oy**-too
nine / ten	*nove / dez*	**naw**-veh / dehsh
How much is it?	*Quanto é?*	**kwahn**-too eh
Write it?	*Escreva?*	ish-**kray**-vah
Is it free?	*É gratis?*	eh **grah**-teesh
Is it included?	*Está incluido?*	ish-**tah** een-kloo-**ee**-doo
Where can I find / buy...?	*Onde posso encontrar / comprar...?*	oh<u>n</u>-deh **paw**-soo ay<u>n</u>-koh<u>n</u>-**trar** / koh<u>n</u>-**prar**
I'd like / We'd like...	*Gostaria / Gostaríamos...*	goosh-tah-**ree**-ah / goosh-tah-**ree**-ah-moosh
...a room.	*...um quarto.*	oo<u>n</u> **kwar**-too
...a ticket to ___.	*...um bilhete para ___.*	oo<u>n</u> beel-**yeh**-teh **pah**-rah ___
Is it possible?	*É possível?*	eh poo-**see**-vehl
Where is...?	*Onde é que é...?*	oh<u>n</u>-deh eh keh eh
...the train station	*...a estação de comboio*	ah ish-tah-**sow** deh koh<u>n</u>-**boy**-yoo
...the bus station	*...a terminal de autocarros*	ah tehr-mee-**nahl** deh ow-too-**kah**-roosh
...the tourist information office	*...a posto de turismo*	ah **poh**-stoo deh too-**reez**-moo
...the toilet	*...a casa de banho*	ah **kah**-zah deh **bahn**-yoo
men	*homens*	**aw**-may<u>n</u>sh
women	*mulheres*	mool-**yeh**-rish
left / right	*esquerda / direita*	ish-**kehr**-dah / dee-**ray**-tah
straight	*em frente*	ay<u>n</u> **frayn**-teh
What time does this open / close?	*As que horas é que abre / fecha?*	ahsh keh **aw**-rahsh eh keh **ah**-breh / **feh**-shah
At what time?	*As que horas?*	ahsh keh **aw**-rahsh
Just a moment.	*Um momento.*	oo<u>n</u> moo-**mayn**-too
now / soon / later	*agora / em breve / mais tarde*	ah-**goh**-rah / ay<u>n</u> **bray**-veh / maish **tar**-deh
today / tomorrow	*hoje / amanhã*	**oh**-zheh / ah-ming-**yah**

PRACTICALITIES

In the Restaurant

English	Portuguese	Pronunciation
I'd like / We'd like...	Gostaria / Gostaríamos...	goosh-tah-**ree**-ah / goosh-tah-**ree**-ah-moosh
...to reserve...	...de reservar...	deh reh-zehr-**var**
...a table for one. / two.	...uma mesa para uma. / duas.	**oo**-mah **may**-zah **pah**-rah **oo**-mah / **doo**-ahsh
Non-smoking.	Não fumar.	no<u>w</u> foo-**mar**
Is this table free?	Esta mesa está livre?	**ehsh**-tah **meh**-zah ish-**tah lee**-vreh
The menu (in English), please.	A ementa (em inglês), por favor.	ah eh-**mayn**-tah (ay<u>n</u> een-**glaysh**) poor fah-vor
service (not) included	serviço (não) incluído	sehr-**vee**-soo (no<u>w</u>) een-kloo-ee-doo
cover charge	coberto	koh-**behr**-too
to go	para fora	**pah**-rah **foh**-rah
with / without	com / sem	koh<u>n</u> / say<u>n</u>
and / or	e / ou	ee / oh
specialty of the house	especialidade da casa	ish-peh-see-ah-lee-**dah**-deh dah **kah**-zah
half portion	meia dose	**may**-ah **doh**-zeh
daily special	prato do dia	**prah**-too doo **dee**-ah
tourist menu	ementa turística	eh-**mayn**-tah too-**reesh**-tee-kah
appetizers	entradas	ay<u>n</u>-**trah**-dahsh
bread / cheese	pão / queijo	pow / **kay**-zhoo
sandwich	sandes	**sahn**-desh
soup / salad	sopa / salada	**soh**-pah / sah-**lah**-dah
meat	carne	**kar**-neh
poultry	aves	**ah**-vish
fish / seafood	peixe / marisco	**pay**-shee / mah-**reesh**-koo
fruit	fruta	**froo**-tah
vegetables	legumes	lay-**goo**-mish
dessert	sobremesa	soo-breh-**may**-zah
tap water	água da torneira	**ah**-gwah dah tor-**nay**-rah
mineral water	água mineral	**ah**-gwah mee-neh-**rahl**
milk	leite	**lay**-teh
(orange) juice	sumo (de laranja)	**soo**-moo (deh lah-**rah<u>n</u>**-zhah)
coffee / tea	café / chá	kah-**feh** / shah
wine	vinho	**veen**-yoo
red / white	tinto / branco	**teen**-too / **brang**-koo
glass / bottle	copo / garrafa	**koh**-poo / gah-**rah**-fah
beer	cerveja	sehr-**vay**-zhah
Cheers!	Saúde!	sah-**oo**-deh
More. / Another.	Mais. / Outro.	maish / **oh**-troo
The same.	O mesmo.	oo **mehsh**-moo
The bill, please.	A conta, por favor.	ah-**kohn**-tah poor fah-**vor**
tip	gorjeta	gor-**zheh**-tah
Delicious!	Delicioso!	deh-lee-see-**oh**-zoo

For many more pages of survival phrases for your trip to Portugal, check out *Rick Steves' Portuguese Phrase Book & Dictionary*.

INDEX

INDEX

Our website enhances this book and turns

Explore Europe

At ricksteves.com you can browse through thousands of articles, videos, photos and radio interviews, plus find a wealth of money-saving travel tips for planning your dream trip. And with our mobile-friendly website, you can easily access all this great travel information anywhere you go.

TV Shows

Preview the places you'll visit by watching entire half-hour episodes of Rick Steves' Europe (choose from all 100 shows) on-demand, for free.

your travel dreams into affordable reality

Radio Interviews

Enjoy ready access to Rick's vast library of radio interviews covering travel

tips and cultural insights that relate specifically to your Europe travel plans.

Travel Forums

Learn, ask, share! Our online community of savvy travelers is a great resource

for first-time travelers to Europe, as well as seasoned pros. You'll find forums on each country, plus travel tips and restaurant/hotel reviews. You can even ask one of our well-traveled staff to chime in with an opinion.

Travel News

Subscribe to our free Travel News e-newsletter, and get monthly updates from Rick on what's happening in Europe.

Rick's Free Travel App

Get your FREE **Rick Steves Audio Europe**™ app to enjoy...

- Dozens of self-guided tours of Europe's top museums, sights and historic walks

- Hundreds of tracks filled with cultural insights and sightseeing tips from Rick's radio interviews

- All organized into handy geographic playlists

- For iPhone, iPad, iPod Touch, Android

With Rick whispering in your ear, Europe gets even better.

Find out more at ricksteves.com

Pack Light and Right

Gear up for your next adventure at ricksteves.com

Light Luggage

Pack light and right with Rick Steves' affordable, custom-designed rolling carry-on bags, backpacks, day packs and shoulder bags.

Accessories

From packing cubes to moneybelts and beyond, Rick has personally selected the travel goodies that will help your trip go smoother.

Rick Steves has

Experience maximum Europe

Save time and energy

This guidebook is your independent-travel toolkit. But for all it delivers, it's still up to you to devote the time and energy it takes to manage the preparation and logistics that are essential for a happy trip. If that's a hassle, there's a solution.

Rick Steves Tours

A Rick Steves tour takes you to Europe's most interesting places with great

with minimum stress

guides and small groups of 28 or less. We follow Rick's favorite itineraries, ride in comfy buses, stay in family-run hotels, and bring you intimately close to the Europe you've traveled so far to see. Most importantly, we take away the logistical headaches so you can focus on the fun.

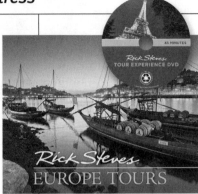

customers—along with us on 40 different itineraries, from Ireland to Italy to Istanbul. Is a Rick Steves tour the right fit for your travel dreams? Find out at ricksteves.com, where you can also get Rick's latest tour catalog and free Tour Experience DVD.

Join the fun

This year we'll take 18,000 free-spirited travelers— nearly half of them repeat

Europe is best experienced with happy travel partners. We hope you can join us.

See our itineraries at ricksteves.com

EUROPE GUIDES

Best of Europe
Eastern Europe
Europe Through the Back Door
Mediterranean Cruise Ports
Northern European Cruise Ports

COUNTRY GUIDES

Croatia & Slovenia
England
France
Germany
Great Britain
Ireland
Italy
Portugal
Scandinavia
Spain
Switzerland

CITY & REGIONAL GUIDES

Amsterdam, Bruges & Brussels
Barcelona
Budapest
Florence & Tuscany
Greece: Athens & the Peloponnese
Istanbul
London
Paris
Prague & the Czech Republic
Provence & the French Riviera
Rome
Venice
Vienna, Salzburg & Tirol

SNAPSHOT GUIDES

Basque Country: Spain & France
Berlin
Bruges & Brussels
Copenhagen & the Best of
    Denmark
Dublin
Dubrovnik
Hill Towns of Central Italy
Italy's Cinque Terre
Krakow, Warsaw & Gdansk
Lisbon
Madrid & Toledo
Milan & the Italian Lakes District
Munich, Bavaria & Salzburg
Naples & the Amalfi Coast
Northern Ireland
Norway
Scotland
Sevilla, Granada & Southern Spain
Stockholm

POCKET GUIDES

Amsterdam
Athens
Barcelona
Florence
London
Paris
Rome
Venice

Rick Steves guidebooks are published by Avalon Travel,
a member of the Perseus Books Group.

NOW AVAILABLE:
eBOOKS, DVD & BLU-RAY

TRAVEL CULTURE

Europe 101
European Christmas
Postcards from Europe
Travel as a Political Act

eBOOKS

Nearly all Rick Steves guides are available as ebooks. Check with your favorite bookseller.

RICK STEVES' EUROPE DVDs

11 New Shows 2013–2014
Austria & the Alps
Eastern Europe
England & Wales
European Christmas
European Travel Skills & Specials
France
Germany, BeNeLux & More
Greece, Turkey & Portugal
Iran
Ireland & Scotland
Italy's Cities
Italy's Countryside
Scandinavia
Spain
Travel Extras

BLU-RAY

Celtic Charms
Eastern Europe Favorites
European Christmas
Italy Through the Back Door
Mediterranean Mosaic
Surprising Cities of Europe

PHRASE BOOKS & DICTIONARIES

French
French, Italian & German
German
Italian
Portuguese
Spanish

JOURNALS

Rick Steves Pocket Travel Journal
Rick Steves Travel Journal

PLANNING MAPS

Britain, Ireland & London
Europe
France & Paris
Germany, Austria & Switzerland
Ireland
Italy
Spain & Portugal

RickSteves.com 📘📷 @RickSteves

Rick Steves books and DVDs are available at bookstores and through online booksellers.

Photo © Patricia Feaster

Avalon Travel
a member of the Perseus Books Group
1700 Fourth Street
Berkeley, CA 94710

Text © 2015 by Rick Steves
Maps © 2015 by Rick Steves' Europe.
Printed in Canada by Friesens. First printing April 2015.

For the latest on Rick Steves' lectures, guidebooks, tours, public radio show, and public
television series, contact Rick Steves' Europe, 130 Fourth Avenue North, Edmonds,
WA 98020, tel. 425/771-8303, www.ricksteves.com, rick@ricksteves.com.
Portions of this book originally appeared in *Rick Steves' Portugal, 8th edition*.

ISBN 978-1-61238-548-8

Rick Steves' Europe

Managing Editor: Risa Laib
Editorial & Production Manager: Jennifer Madison Davis
Editors: Glenn Eriksen, Tom Griffin, Cameron Hewitt, Suzanne Kotz, Cathy Lu,
    Carrie Shepherd
Editorial & Production Assistant: Jessica Shaw
Editorial Interns: Stacie Larsen, Mallory Presho-Dunne
Researcher: Robert Wright
Maps & Graphics: David C. Hoerlein, Sandra Hundacker, Lauren Mills, Mary Rostad

Avalon Travel

Senior Editor and Series Manager: Madhu Prasher
Editor: Jamie Andrade
Associate Editor: Maggie Ryan
Copy Editor: Judith Brown
Proofreader: Kelly Lydick
Indexer: Stephen Callahan
Production & Typesetting: Tabitha Lahr, Rue Flaherty, Christine DeLorenzo
Cover Design: Kimberly Glyder Design
Maps & Graphics: Kat Bennett, Mike Morgenfeld

Photo Credits

Front Cover: Lisbon © Carlos Caetano/Dreamstime.com
Title Page: Pena Palace in Sintra © Rui Vale de Sousa/123rf.com
Chapter Openers: p. 1, Salema; p. 17, View from Largo Santa Luzia, Lisbon; p. 121,
    National Palace, Sintra; p. 137, Algarve Beach; p. 179, Roman Temple, Évora; p. 202,
    View of Nazaré from Sítio; p. 240, Coimbra Street Scene; p. 274, Ponte Dom Luís I;
    p. 318, Douro Valley View; p. 336, Monuments to the Discoveries, Lisbon
Additional Photography: Dominic Bonuccelli, Rich Earl, Cameron Hewitt, David C.
    Hoerlein, Carol Ries, Jennifer Schutte, Robyn Stencil, Rick Steves, Ashley Sytsma,
    Robert Wright, Reid Coen, Wikimedia Commons—PD-Art/PD-US (photos are
    used by permission and are the property of the original copyright owners)

ABOUT THE AUTHOR

RICK STEVES

 Since 1973, Rick Steves has spent 100 days every year exploring Europe. Along with writing and researching a bestselling series of guidebooks, Rick produces a public television series *(Rick Steves' Europe)*, a public radio show *(Travel with Rick Steves)*, a blog on Facebook, and an app and podcast *(Rick Steves Audio Europe);* writes a nationally syndicated newspaper column; organizes guided tours that more than 20,000 travelers to Europe annually; and offers an information-packed website (www.ricksteves.com). With the help of his hardworking staff of 100 at Rick Steves' Europe—in Edmonds, Washington, just north of Seattle—Rick's mission is to make European travel fun, affordable, and culturally enlightening for Americans.

Connect with Rick:

f facebook.com/RickSteves   twitter: @RickSteves